Stand Hunting for
WHITETAILS

Richard P. Smith

© 1996 by

Richard P. Smith

Published by

**krause
publications**

700 E. State Street • Iola, WI 54990-0001
Telephone: 715/445-2214

Please call or write for our free catalog of outdoor publications.
Our toll-free number to place an order or obtain a free catalog is 800-258-0929
or please use our regular business telephone 715-445-2214
for editorial comment and further information.

Library of Congress Catalog Number: 95-82427
ISBN: 0-87341-439-X

Printed in the United States of America

Dedication

For George and Bruce: a couple of the best
stand hunting partners a guy could ask for!

Table of Contents

Acknowledgments

There's a long list of people whom I would like to thank for their role in helping me to learn about and enjoy *Stand Hunting for Whitetails* across North America. Many of the most important lessons were learned during the early years in Michigan while hunting with Uncle George and my brother Bruce. George made it possible for my brother and I to hunt whitetails and learn about them far more than we would have been able otherwise.

Even when we no longer hunted together, we always shared deer hunting experiences during visits or over the telephone. Unfortunately, that sharing will no longer be possible because George passed away during early December of 1995. He was deer hunting at the time, making a drive for his son Craig when he suffered a fatal heart attack.

George enjoyed deer hunting, especially when hunting from a stand, and he passed that enjoyment on to Bruce and I, his son and some of his son's friends. Most of George's whitetails were shot while stand hunting, including his last. It was a nice 6-pointer that he dropped during the morning of November 15, 1995, opening day of Michigan's gun season.

I've been fortunate enough to be a guest in many a fine deer hunting camp, and I have enjoyed some exceptional stand hunts for whitetails courtesy of my hosts. They include Bill Jordan of Columbus, Georgia, who developed the Realtree Camo Patterns; Callaway Gardens at Pine Mountain, Georgia; Tony Knight and Toby Bridges with Modern Muzzleloading; Greg and Paul Bambenek with Dr. Juice Scents; the Markesbery Brothers (Russ, Rick and Chris) with Rusty Duck Gun Care Products; Brent Hunt of South Carolina, manufacturer of Trophy Whitetail Tree Stands; Bob Eastman and George Gardner of The Game Tracker Company; Bear Archery Company; Ottie Snyder Jr., Mark Bower and Dave Ford with Horton Manufacturing; Hayward Simmons with the Cedar Knoll Hunt Club in South Carolina; Alabama's Charles Dixon, who operates a bow and gun camp near Selma; Greg Simons in Texas (San Angelo), fellow outdoor writer John Weiss in Ohio, Pat Durkin and Debbie Knauer, Editor and Publisher of *Deer & Deer Hunting Magazine*; Al Hofacker, Cofounder and Former Editor of *Deer & Deer Hunting Magazine*; John Bardahl and Mike Aftanas with Proud Foot Creek Outfitters in Saskatchewan; and Buddy Chudy of Mantagao Outfitters in Manitoba.

Some other individuals whom I would like to thank for their help during stand hunts for whitetails are Jimmy Dean, Joe Drake, Chuck Jones, hunting consultant Bill Whitfield from San Antonio, Tom Fegely, Ted Humphreys, David Blanton, Vicki Skeeters, Marv Briegel, Ronnie Groom, Larry Weishuhn, Kent Horner, Andy Dunnaway, Rick and Ricky C. Smith from Pennsylvania, Jim Butler, Dave Raikko, Jim Haveman, Dave Larsen, Brad Rucks, Doug Leitch, Dick Johnson and Dan Vander Sys. I also want to thank the many friends, relatives and fellow hunters who have allowed me to be a part of their hunts in some way, shape or form, especially those who were patient enough to allow me to take photographs and answer my many questions.

Lucy, my wife and business partner, also deserves plenty of credit for the help she provided in producing this book. She helped with research, proofreading and editing the manuscript and the layout of the front and back covers. Her assistance was invaluable.

A big thanks is also due Deborah Faupel at Krause Publications for her tremendous patience in allowing me the time I needed to complete this project.

Some of the chapters in this book were originally published as articles in *Petersen's Bowhunting, Buckmasters, North American Whitetail, Whitetail Strategies* and *Deer & Deer Hunting Magazines* and the permission to reprint them with revisions is gratefully acknowledged.

Introduction

The authors and editors of dictionaries are behind the times when it comes to whitetail hunting. *Stand Hunting for Whitetails* is the most popular and productive method of connecting on this species of deer over most of their range, which covers much of North America. Yet, I can't find a definition in a dictionary that describes this form of hunting under the words *hunt* or *hunting*. I will try to help them out by providing my definition of this tactic, as it relates to whitetail hunting, of course.

Stand Hunting: 1: a form of hunting during which a hunter occupies a tree stand, an elevated platform, a ground blind or utilizes natural cover to wait for whitetails to appear; 2: waiting in ambush; 3: hiding from deer to avoid detection; 4: allowing game to come to the hunter; 5: the art of selecting a spot from which whitetails can be ambushed.

Stand Hunting for Whitetails is certainly nothing new. I've been doing it for the thirty years I've been hunting whitetails and I'm sure there are deer hunters out there who have been doing it longer. However, stand hunting has grown in popularity during recent years and a number of factors are responsible for that.

For one thing, whitetails are more widespread and abundant than they have ever been before, giving more people in more places the opportunity to hunt them. The increasing popularity of bowhunting for whitetails has drawn more hunters to the stand hunting fold because this is the best technique available for consistently getting shots at deer within bow range. Stand hunting is actually the best means of consistently getting good shots at whitetails regardless of what hunters choose to hunt with.

Changes in land ownership, usage and access have also been major factors in increasing the popularity of stand hunting. There are far fewer areas today than there used to be where deer hunters can roam freely over large tracts of land while stillhunting, conducting drives or snow tracking whitetails. In fact, many of today's whitetail hunters hunt on parcels that are forty acres or less in size. It doesn't take a large chunk of land to stand hunt effectively.

I've been extremely successful while stand hunting for whitetails across North America and I've interviewed many other hunters who have been more successful. If you are interested in becoming a stand hunter or want to become better at it, this book should help you along. The information on the pages that follow might not answer all of your questions, but you should find the answers to most of them. And, more importantly, reading this book should help you learn how to tag more whitetails while stand hunting.

Chapter 1

Why Hunt from a Stand/Blind?

My best whitetail to date will help illustrate the value of stand hunting. It was a big-bodied Canadian buck with a heavy, non-typical 12-point rack that I shot with a muzzleloader. The date was October 28th and I was occupying a stand in a white birch tree on a ridge overlooking a valley. Another ridge was across the valley about 100 yards away.

Fresh snow had fallen overnight in conjunction with a cold front, increasing visibility. The brown coats of whitetails would be easy to see

My best whitetail was taken from a tree stand with a Knight muzzleloader in Saskatchewan during October of 1993. The non-typical 12-pointer had a drop tine and a gross score of 175 6/8, netting 165 6/8.

My best whitetail taken while hunting from the ground was a Michigan 11-pointer that netted 148 4/8. The trophy buck made a death run after being shot through the lungs. He ended up with his head draped over a fallen tree, as shown in this picture.

against the white background. The temperature had been in the 40s the day before, but was 18 degrees Fahrenheit that morning with a significant wind chill.

During the afternoon, a doe and fawn suddenly came running into view on the ridge across the valley. My first thought was that they might have winded me, but the wind wasn't blowing that way. Then it occurred to me that a buck might have rousted them out. The thought barely flashed through my mind when a thick-necked, dark-antlered whitetail materialized behind them.

I had been hoping for at least a good 8-point. It was immediately obvious that this buck exceeded my minimum, so I grabbed my rifle and prepared for a shot. I had sighted the front loader in for one hundred yards, so I was confident of making the shot. Soon after I shouldered the rifle, the deer stopped broadside in an opening. I put the crosshairs on his shoulder and squeezed the trigger.

Once I made the decision to shoot, I ignored the buck's antlers. I knew he was a good one, but I was in for a surprise when I walked up to him. The rack was more massive than I thought and I had no idea the antlers had a drop tine. What a thrill it was realizing I had taken a nice non-typical! The rack had a gross score of 175 6/8 and the huge whitetail had a dressed weight of 235 pounds.

There's no question in my mind that stand hunting was the best way to connect on such a fine buck and the same thing is true across most of the whitetail's range in North America. Had I been walking instead of waiting, there's an excellent chance that buck would have learned about my presence in the same way I learned about his. My movement could have spooked the doe and fawn and they, in turn, would have alerted that buck and possibly others in the area.

Although it is true stand hunting can be more effective than walking or stillhunting, on that particular hunt I didn't have any other option. I was hunting in Saskatchewan where, as a nonresident from another country, I was required to hunt with a guide. Regulations in that province limit hunters like me to hunting from a fixed position, whether in a tree or on the ground, unless in the company of a guide. Most guides have too many duties to spend all day with one hunter and my guide on that hunt was no exception.

I'm not complaining, of course. I'm just pointing out why my options were limited on that hunt, and that other United States residents who hunt in that province will encounter the same thing. If given a choice, I usually prefer waiting for whitetails to come to me rather than trying to go to them. I hunt from elevated stands whenever possible, but I've taken plenty of good bucks from the ground, too, either while occupying a blind or relying on natural cover.

My best buck from a ground-based post, for example, was another trophy whitetail. It had a typical 11-point rack and was 5 1/2 years old. That deer came from a remote section of Michigan's Upper Peninsula on November 16th, the second day of gun season. I was watching what appeared to be a breeding area at the time.

The spot consisted of a small clearing in a stand of mature hardwood trees. There were several large balsam fir trees in the clearing and a group of young balsams along one side. One end of the oval-shaped clearing was covered with scrapes. I counted nine of them. Most of the pawings were small to average in size, but several were larger than average. I didn't measure their dimensions, but they were roughly four feet long by two feet wide.

I posted next to a large hardwood tree fifty yards downwind from the scrapes with my .30-06. That spot gave me the best vantage point of the scrapes and my surroundings. The tree trunk helped break my outline.

Things got off to a good start on the 16th when a yearling 3-pointer checked the scrapes at 9:05 a.m. and I passed him up. Seven hours and ten minutes later, the trophy buck appeared, coming from the opposite direction of the young deer. The large set of antlers that adorned the mature buck's head caught my attention immediately. The whitetail was walking broadside to me about thirty-five yards away and had no idea I was there. When the crosshairs were on his shoulder, I tripped the trigger.

Although solidly hit through the lungs, the deer broke into a death run and I heard him crash into a group of trees seconds later. Unfortunately, he broke the tip off of one of his tines during the collision, preventing the antlers from netting in the 150s. The final official net score was 148 4/8, a fitting reward for sticking with stand hunting and an excellent incentive for continuing to use the technique. And one of the ways for you to take some of the best bucks in your area is to try this method.

Stand hunting is not just for hunters interested in big bucks, of course. It's a method that's well-suited for taking bucks and does of all sizes. The technique is ideal for use by any and all hunters from the very young to the very old. It also allows hunters who are handicapped to be able to hunt.

Stand hunting is a perfect way to introduce a youngster to deer hunting. An adult who shares a blind or stand with the beginner can coach them along, giving them pointers that will serve them well when they occupy a stand on their own. Ambushing whitetails from a blind is also an excellent way for oldsters to carry on a tradition they may have participated in all of their lives.

Besides the fact anyone can successfully hunt whitetails from a blind or stand, it's an easy method to master compared to other tech-

Stand hunting is a perfect way to introduce youngsters to deer hunting. They can either post on their own or be accompanied by an adult who can coach them. In this photo Jim Haveman is shown stand hunting with his daughter Kortney as they take advantage of natural cover as a blind.

niques. It's simply a matter of sitting and waiting as still and as quietly as possible until a deer comes along. There's actually more to it than that, all of which will be expanded upon in each chapter of this book; however, that's the basic principle involved. Most hunters don't have difficulty mastering stand hunting, at least for short spans of time.

The element of surprise is one of the most important factors whitetail hunters can have in their favor when it comes to seeing a deer they want to shoot and being able to follow through on that intention. When a buck or doe doesn't know a hunter is within gun or bow range, the hunter has a better opportunity to wait for the best possible shot and to make a clean kill. There is no better way I know of to consistently take advantage of that element of surprise than to wait for whitetails from a properly placed stand or blind.

Based on thirty years of experience hunting whitetails, I discovered it's far easier to go undetected when allowing deer to come to me than trying to sneak up on them. In most cases, the latter simply doesn't work. Wild whitetails don't like being approached by people or any other potential predator and their superior senses enable them to detect most moving hunters long before hunters are able to see deer.

14-year-old Perry Brown with his first white-tail taken from a tree stand while hunting South Carolina's Cedar Knoll Hunt Club on August 15. Anyone can successfully hunt deer from stands, including the young, the old and handicapped.

In fact, the first clue walking hunters most often get that whitetails are in the vicinity is the sound of a snort or pounding hooves accompanied by a flash of movement or a waving white tail as the animals vacate the premises. The less than stealthy attributes of most hunters, myself included, don't help matters. If we were meant to travel through thickets with the same stealth that whitetails possess, we would be walking on four legs and have a natural fur coat.

I don't mean to imply that it's impossible to get the drop on whitetails while stillhunting or stalking because I've done it and I know there are plenty of hunters who are better at it than me. My point is that posted hunters will get the opportunity to accurately determine the size and sex of deer they see and will be in a better position to kill the animals they decide to take, more often than hunters who are using a different technique. There are probably more whitetails shot from tree stands and ground blinds than any other hunting method. In the vast majority of those cases, the deer had no idea a hunter was in the area until it was too late.

The element of surprise is far more important for bow hunters than those using firearms because most whitetails are shot at distances less than 30 yards. I would hazard a guess that at least 90 percent of the whitetails tagged by archers are shot from stands or blinds. The Michigan Bowhunters Association maintains records on how deer were taken in the state. During recent years more than 90 percent of the whitetails were shot from tree stands or ground blinds.

Pope and Young Club records for the 19th recording period (1993-94) show that 90 percent of the 2,793 whitetails entered were shot from tree stands or ground blinds. Eighty-one percent were arrowed from tree stands and 6.5 percent were shot from ground blinds. Another two percent fell to archers who were calling and .75 percent were taken by hunters using bait, both of which are forms of stand hunting.

The majority of whitetails taken by bowhunters every year are arrowed from tree stands. This archer is in a ladder stand with a camouflaged covering to reduce the chances of the hunter being seen.

The majority of whitetails tagged by gun hunters every year are also taken from stands/blinds.

The percentage of whitetails claimed by gun hunters from ambush probably also represents a majority of the deer bagged each year, with figures of 70 to 80 percent being reasonable. More than 95 percent of the whitetails I've shot over the years with both gun and bow have been killed while I was posted. Most of my deer hunting has been spent waiting for whitetails to come to me, not because I always enjoy that method the most, but because I have been most consistently successful that way and so have many other whitetail hunters. You can be, too.

There are a number of reasons why stand hunting is so effective when it's done right. Most importantly, the proper use of a ground blind or tree stand prevents whitetails from smelling or seeing hunters. At the same time, hunters often have a good view of any deer that wander by. When the time is right, those circumstances allow hunters to make the best shot possible.

Many hunters prefer to ambush whitetails from elevated stands because it reduces their chances of being smelled and seen, and because it improves visibility for the hunter. Hunters in tree stands versus ground blinds are actually on equal footing when it comes to being winded by whitetails, as long as both are downwind from where deer are. The elevated hunter has a slight advantage, however, in situations where animals appear downwind from the hunter's position. Scent from a person in a tree may blow or drift over those deer, but that seldom happens when hunters are on the ground.

Ground based hunters in blinds have just as good a chance of going unseen by whitetails as hunters in tree stands, as long as the blind provides adequate concealment and the occupant is not backlit or silhouetted. It's also important for stand hunters to avoid making any suspicious sounds that might draw attention to themselves. An out-of-place noise can be enough to send a cautious whitetail on its way, even if it doesn't see any thing out of the ordinary.

Ground-based hunters with little or no cover are at a definite disadvantage compared to those in elevated positions. Deer are quick to pick up the movement associated with raising a rifle or drawing a bow, unless it's done when the animal's head is turned away or behind a tree. Whitetails are not as good at spotting movement above them as they are at ground level, and that gives hunters perched in trees an advantage. It's not true, however, that deer never look up. That trait may have been poorly developed before tree stands became popular, but during recent years more and more bucks and does are making it a habit to look for danger from above.

When it comes to visibility, tree stand users have their biggest edge over hunters hoping to ambush a whitetail from the ground. An elevated position often, but not always, makes it possible to see deer sooner and at greater distances than from a ground position. Another benefit is the ability to shoot over limbs and brush.

Stand hunting also allows the best use of a human's keenest senses: hearing and eyesight. Remaining motionless in a fixed position not only reduces the chances that deer will detect us, it increases our chances of sensing them. Whitetails on the prowl are more visible because their movement gives them away. And they often make noise, too, but not always.

As far as being able to see or hear a whitetail, a hunter who is moving is at a disadvantage compared to the hunter who is sitting. It's impossible to avoid making occasional noises while walking, which can either cover up or distract from sounds that

Both gun and bowhunters who spend time in tree stands often have better visibility than those on the ground. They are less likely to be smelled by deer downwind of them, too.

might be made by a deer. And the sneaking hunter is constantly looking at different settings, making it difficult to sometimes notice small things that might be part of a whitetail's anatomy. The vigilant stand hunter's constant monitoring of the setting will enable them to notice subtle changes.

Those same factors that hamper a moving hunter's ability to see or hear a deer increase a whitetail's chances of pinpointing the presence and location of an intruder. The stillhunter also spreads more scent over a larger area, making it easier for deer to smell him or her.

Comfort is one more consideration in favor of stand hunting, especially when weather conditions are trying. It's tough to beat an enclosed blind for comfort when it's raining, windy and/or cold. Blinds that come with heaters can be a major benefit during cold conditions. Outfitter Buddy Chudy from Winnipeg, Manitoba, makes homemade tree stands with portable heaters that fit under swivel seats. Even though the top of the stands are open, the heaters generate enough heat to keep the lower body and hands warm, which is a major benefit.

Stand hunting is also the best option when the weather is hot in the south or even up north during early seasons. It's far more comfortable and tolerable to sit somewhere in the shade and be as cool as possible while you wait for a whitetail to come to you rather than working up a sweat in the process of trying to find a deer. When the ground is carpeted with a layer of noisy leaves or crunchy snow, stand hunting is usually the best choice, too. It's better to listen to the sounds of whitetails moving your way than

Tim Wolf blows a deer call from one of Buddy Chudy's heated tree stands in Manitoba.

Ground blinds such as this Senco Super Blind often offer more comfort than tree stands during inclement weather. They are also safer.

to hear the loud crackle and crunch of every footstep you take.

In the following chapters, you will be reading more about my two best bucks taken from stands. I will highlight appropriate information about those kills and what led to them. There will be plenty of information about other deer I've taken over the years, too, as well as anecdotes from family, friends and acquaintances.

Most importantly, by the time you finish reading this book you will have a solid grasp of what's involved in stand hunting. You will learn how to use this method most effectively through examples from my experience, as well as the experiences of many other hunters. Mistakes will be mentioned in addition to things that were done right. In my opinion, one of the best ways to learn is from those who have done it.

Chapter 2

Selecting Stand Sites

Wherever and whenever there's a bumper crop of acorns, it's tough for a whitetail hunter to go wrong by stand hunting in or near the area where the mast crop is located. Plenty of deer are sure to be nearby because acorns are the number one natural food of whitetails. Although beechnuts are also near the top of the list, beech trees are not as prevalent as oaks. By posting along a major trail leading to and from a stand of oak trees or at a spot overlooking the food supply, hunters are sure to get a look at some of the deer using the area and should be able to connect if the right one comes along.

Selecting stand sites in or near oak trees when acorns are abundant is a good strategy. Stands can be positioned where whitetails are eating the nuts or along trails leading to and from feeding areas.

My most recent experience with hunting whitetails in the oaks came during a December hunt on the Encinitos Ranch in south Texas. Until then I didn't realize oak trees grew that far south, but it was a pleasant surprise when I found out they produced an abundant supply of acorns that year. As it turned out, it had been at least four years since the live oak trees on the 40,000-acre ranch near McAllen had produced a mast crop. The hot, dry climate of south Texas doesn't often generate enough rainfall for acorn production, but a sufficient amount of rain fell during 1994 for the trees to develop a bumper crop of nuts, and local whitetails were taking advantage of the abundant food source.

Oak groves only make up a small portion of the habitat on the Encinitos. Most of the ranch is brush country, which is composed primarily of mesquite, cactus and weeds. The thick brush normally harbors a lot of whitetails, but more deer than normal were being drawn into the oaks to feed on acorns.

I jumped at the chance to hunt an oak grove from a camouflaged ground blind. Hunting from the ground was the best choice because most trees weren't big enough for stands and the visibility was better from ground level. Posting in the oaks proved to be a good decision because during the hunt I enjoyed some of the best whitetail action in terms of total deer and buck sightings. I not only saw a lot of whitetails, but they were active in the oaks during much of the day.

Two other factors helped boost deer activity while I hunted in Texas. A cold front blew in soon after my arrival and the rut was starting to get underway. The peak of whitetail breeding occurs during December and January in Texas due to its latitude.

I was part of a group of writers Bill Jordan had invited to hunt the Encinitos. Jordan hosts an outdoor television show called "Realtree Outdoors" that is aired on the TNN Network and he hoped to have his crew film some segments for the show during the hunt. When we arrived in McAllen on the afternoon of December 9th, the temperature was in the 80s and the weather had been hot for weeks, but by the time we reached the ranch two hours later, the temperature had dropped to the 50s.

Hunt coordinator Bill Whitfield told us the change in weather would increase deer activity along with our chances for success. Before the front moved out two days later, temperatures dropped as low as the 30s. A blast of cold air like that at the right time often triggers rut-related buck activity, which it did.

I saw 16 bucks and countless does during the first day of hunting. Most of the bucks I got a good look at had average 8-point racks. However, a buck that I think had a better rack slipped across a sendero about 125 yards to my left before I was able to see how big his antlers were.

The blind I was in was positioned along the edge of a narrow trail or lane through the oaks, which are called senderos. I could watch for deer crossing the sendero to my left and right. Whitetails moving through the oaks were visible in front of and behind me.

About an hour after daylight on the second day of hunting I heard a pair of bucks sparring in the oaks behind me and to the right. Not long afterward, two large antlered bucks crossed the sendero to my right more than 100 yards away. Like the decent buck I saw the day before, they crossed the lane before I had time to get a good look at them.

It wasn't long before bucks started chasing does. At one point a trio of 8-pointers were after the same doe. By noon I had seen a pair of mature bucks feed on acorns in front of me, but I passed them up, hoping to see something better.

One of a number of bucks I passed up while hunting the oaks from a ground blind in Texas during December. I now think this buck had a better rack than the one I shot.

One of those bucks had a wide 8-point rack with a pair of non-typical points sprouting near the base of one of the beams, making him a 10-point. The second decent buck had what would have been a beautifully symmetrical 10-point rack, except one of the brow tines was broken off near the base. I would have shot that deer if it weren't for the broken tine.

I finally did fill my tag with a third good buck that appeared on the edge of the sendero to my left at 4:15 p.m. The buck showed up in about the same place as the one that had slipped by me the day before, but this time he stopped long enough for me to get my crosshairs on him. I could see five points on his left antler and I thought the right beam had the same number of points, so I squeezed the trigger.

The buck proved to be a 9-pointer, but I was pleased nonetheless. It was a fine Texas whitetail taken while hunting in the oaks much the same way I've taken many midwestern whitetails. For more information about deer hunting on the Encinitos Ranch and other locations

I admire a 9-point buck (that I thought was a 10) that I ended up shooting while hunting an oak grove in Texas. The trees are live oaks. Enough rain had fallen on the Encinitos Ranch during 1994 to produce a bumper crop of acorns. It had been at least four years since the last crop of the nuts.

in Texas contact Bill Whitfield, 3003 Low Oak, San Antonio, TX 78232 (210-494-6421).

Since I was hunting with a rifle in that case, it was beneficial to hunt from the ground where I had the best visibility of as much area as possible. Had I been hunting with bow and arrow, it would have been better to select a spot for an ambush that would have put me within bow range of feeding deer or those moving to and from the oaks on a runway. To determine where deer are feeding in the oaks, look for pawed leaves and an accumulation of droppings.

Pay attention to the direction most deer tracks are heading on trails to determine which are used by whitetails on the way to feed and those leading toward bedding areas. Runways used to reach feeding grounds are most productive during afternoons and evenings while those leaving feeding areas often produce the most action during mornings. Getting as close to bedding areas as possible is recommended for morning hunts. Sneaking into position before daylight is also a good idea. Trails that receive deer traffic going both ways can be good at any time and the same is true for blinds or stands overlooking feeding areas. On the Texas hunt, I saw whitetails eating acorns all day long.

White oak acorns are favored by whitetails over red oaks. The leaves of white oaks have rounded lobes as shown here.

You should select locations for blinds or stands that are downwind from where you expect deer to be. If setting up along a trail, position yourself near a jog in the trail so whitetails will be angling away from you, allowing you a clear shot. Twenty yards is an ideal distance for a bow shot, but setting up further away can be better because the chances of being detected by a whitetail are reduced.

When scouting for a stand site overlooking feeding activity, take time to make sure acorns still remain in the area. Once deer eat all of the available acorns they may not return to that spot, preferring to go where nuts remain. Where more than one type of acorns are present, set up near the nuts they prefer. Acorns from white oaks are favored by whitetails over those from the

Leaves and nuts from a red oak tree. Red oak leaves have pointed lobes.

red oak family. Leaves on white oak trees have rounded lobes and the tips of leaves in the red oak family are pointed.

Selecting spots for blinds and stands at or near other feeding areas used by whitetails can be accomplished in much the same way it's done when hunting acorns. Keep the following key elements in mind when doing so - effective range of the gun or bow you're using, wind direction, visibility, concealment and points of concentrated deer activity. Availability of suitable trees to put stands in can be a consideration, too, but it doesn't have to be if you have access to self-supporting models such as tripod stands.

I enjoyed an excellent hunt from a Warren and Sweat tripod along a Nebraska river bottom during November of 1994 with Knight rifle designer Tony Knight and North American Hunting Club Executive Director Bill Miller. We were all using Knight muzzleloaders designed by Tony and hunted on land owned by Marv Briegel. He did a super job setting up the stands.

The tripod I hunted from was positioned next to a large cottonwood tree to help the structure and me blend in. The stand was in an opening on the opposite side of an old river channel from a soybean field. The bean field was to the north of me and woods were to the south. The river channel ran east and west and was a perfect corridor for whitetails that wanted to travel either direction.

The stand was in an opening about 150 yards wide and 75 yards deep. A number of deer trails crossed the opening that whitetails used to travel to and from the bean field. It was an ideal setup. A swivel seat on top of the tripod permitted me to watch all around. A padded rifle rest was another important feature that increased my chances of making an accurate shot when the time came.

I saw lots of deer, including seven bucks, on opening morning as they moved from the bean field to the woods. One of the bucks was a real whopper that I should have gotten, but he caught me by surprise. I had been looking to the

Tony Knight in the tripod stand from which I shot my Nebraska 10-pointer.

north for deer leaving the bean field and when I turned back to the south in the swivel seat, the trophy buck was standing broadside about 80 yards away.

My movement caught his attention and as I started to raise my Knight Legend muzzleloader, he began walking away. I found the wide-antlered 10-pointer in my scope just before he entered the woods, but, unsure of making a killing shot, held my fire.

Five minutes later, I heard a rifle report in the direction the buck had gone and was sure another hunter had claimed the whitetail. My suspicions were confirmed the following day when I saw the buck in the back of a pickup truck owned by Charles Hermes from Hastings, Nebraska. He was obviously pleased the buck made it by me.

The animal's antlers had a net green score of 157 7/8, making it Hermes' highest scoring buck. Before the hunt was over, I would learn that bucks like that aren't unusual in southern Nebraska along the Republican River. Two days later, Tony claimed a 14-pointer that had an even bigger rack. A number of years earlier, Marv bagged a typical 12-pointer on his property that qualified for Boone and Crockett Records, scoring 172.

Four of the six bucks I saw before the big one were small-to-average 8-pointers that I passed up. The other two had larger racks, but they were either too far away or in brush too thick for good visibility. It was 9:15 a.m. when that big 10-pointer got by me.

That evening I connected on another 10-pointer as it chased a doe about 70 yards away. That buck's rack had 6 points on one beam and 4 on the other. It wasn't as big as the one that got away, but it was still a nice whitetail.

Nebraska only has a limited number of nonresident gun deer licenses that are available on a first come, first served basis after resident licenses are issued. However, an unlimited number of licenses are available for the state's December muzzleloader season. Scope-mounted rifles cannot be used during the black powder season.

Although a bigger buck got away, I was pleased with the 10-point buck I bagged with my Knight muzzleloader in Nebraska.

Look for funnels or bottlenecks created by beaver ponds like this one—as well as lakes, fields, rock walls and other types of obstructions to deer movement—when selecting stand sites.

Best hunting in Nebraska is on private land. Public land is limited in the state. For more information about whitetail hunting in Nebraska write to Game and Parks Commission, P.O. Box 30370, Lincoln, NE 68503.

Some excellent spots to keep in mind as possible stand sites are fencelines, funnels or bottlenecks and saddles. Farmland whitetails often follow fencelines or irrigation ditches, favoring some over others. Narrow strips of woods or other types of cover that funnel traveling deer through an area can be super spots for stands. Saddles are low areas in ridgelines that are a type of funnel because whitetails often use them when crossing a ridge to reduce their visibility. Bottlenecks are also a form of funnel created where two lakes or beaver ponds come close together, for example, so whitetails that want to go around them have to go through the bottleneck between the bodies of water or other obstructions.

Ambushing whitetails at or near feeding areas works better early in the season than later. As the season progresses, deer may not reach the dinner table until after dark. In heavily hunted areas, that may be true during the first part of the season, too. Under those circumstances, it's important to select stand sites along routes deer use to reach feeding areas where the deer will be visible during legal shooting time.

Locations in or near thick cover are often good bets, even though visibility is reduced, because whitetails feel most comfortable traveling in security cover during hours of daylight.

Any type of agricultural field can be a virtual whitetail magnet just like that Nebraska soybean field was. Corn and other grain fields are especially attractive to whitetails, too. Keep in mind that deer find a cornfield that has just been picked almost irresistible and the same thing may also apply to other farm fields. Cornfields are often used by whitetails as bedding as well as feeding areas, so posting near a cornfield when it's being picked can also pay off as deer leave the corn for other cover.

Posting near any type of agricultural field such as corn can also be productive.

Selecting stand sites near bedding areas can be productive. The trick is to get in position before the deer do.

Wooded bedding grounds are always good early morning ambush points. Whitetail beds are oval-shaped areas where vegetation is flattened from a deer's weight. Beds are easiest to spot in the snow, but hunters who look carefully should recognize the shallow depressions where whitetails have lain in any type of habitat when snow is absent. Small- and adult-size beds near one another are often those of a doe with her young. Bucks normally make the biggest beds.

A number of beds will be present in favored bedding areas. These locations are usually in heavy cover where the animals aren't often disturbed, but in agricultural areas where there are a lot of fields and not much woods, an increasing number of bucks are bedding in fields where vegetation is high enough to screen them from view. A concentration of antler rubs can be a tip-off to the presence of a buck's bedroom.

Careful scouting is required to locate bedding areas that are used consistently. Wooded terrain will have to be searched thoroughly on foot. In open country, binoculars or spotting scopes can be used from vantage points to pinpoint possible bedding areas by watching deer. Visits to bedding areas should be kept to a minimum to prevent the deer you're after from changing locations. Spring is an excellent time to search out bedding areas because most sign from the previous fall will still be visible. Preseason scouting is the next best option, but if you stumble upon or learn about a bedding area while hunting, that knowledge can also be used to your advantage.

One December a college professor who is a friend of mine, Dr. William Robinson, found a late season bedding area while hunting with bow and arrow. He saw two bucks, one of which was a trophy 10-pointer, and he got a shot at it, but missed. Muzzleloader season was also open at the time, but the next day was the last day of the season. Bill couldn't hunt that day, but he knew I would be, so he told me about the bedding area and how to get to it.

By first light the next morning, I was where he told me to go. I didn't see the big buck he missed, but when a spikehorn showed up about 9:00 a.m., I decided to use my tag on him.

Select ambush sites at or near bedding grounds that will put you downwind from approaching whitetails. It's important to be in position before deer arrive, if possible, which usually means before first light. However, jumped deer that haven't been hunted in their bedroom before may return within a reasonable period of time.

After getting in position at least two hours before daylight, veteran bowhunter Jimmy Dean ambushed a Montana trophy buck one fall in its bedding area. He had to climb a tree he selected for his stand that early because

Veteran bowhunter Jimmy Dean ambushed a trophy Montana whitetail in its bedding area one year by getting in position two hours before daylight. He used a tree sling to hunt from.

he knew the buck got there before daylight, and he wanted to make sure he arrived before the buck. He was hunting from a tree sling and took a nap after securing himself in place.

As expected, it was dark when the buck reached his bedroom. Jimmy woke up to the sounds of the buck's arrival. Content that the buck didn't know he was there, he nodded off again until it got light. When the time was right, he sent an arrow into the whitetail.

In many cases, it may be more practical to select a morning stand between bedding and feeding areas. Bedding grounds can be hard to pinpoint and you want to avoid the risk of causing deer to shift bedding areas. I set up between bedding and feeding areas on a hunt a number of years ago when I had permission to hunt private farm land that was loaded with whitetails. There was a large hay field that attracted a lot of feeding whitetails where I was hunting. A long, narrow patch of plowed ground with woods on both sides led to the middle of the hay field.

Some deer followed the edges of the plowed ground toward bedding areas when they left the field in the morning. However, I didn't know how far deer followed the plowed opening before entering the woods, so on my first morning hunt I selected a spot to wait about 250 yards from the hay field and 20 yards from the edge of the plowed ground. The wind was in my favor, blowing from the open lane toward me.

Within an hour, deer were coming my way, but they turned into the woods before reaching me. When nothing else came along, I made preparations for the next morning's hunt by choosing an ambush site that would put me within striking distance of whitetails vacating the hay field. My stand selection was perfect, but my shooting wasn't as good.

A spike buck came walking along the edge of the opening after daylight the following morning and stopped in an excellent position for a shot. I guessed the distance at 20 yards and aimed accordingly, but my arrow went low. The young buck was further than I thought.

This example illustrates the importance of flexibility when it comes to stand site selection. If the location you choose at first does not work out as expected, use the information about deer movements gathered while waiting there, to move to a better spot. And if the wind switches from one day to the next, be ready to change places to reduce the chances of being smelled by approaching whitetails.

Isolating stand sites that might be best for intercepting a buck is often easiest during early stages of the rut when rubs and scrapes start appearing, unless you've already done so in the spring. Rubs and scrapes made the previous fall remain visible until green-up. Look for concentrations of rubs and scrapes where anxious bucks have left their mark. Antlers are used to skin bark from saplings or small trees to make rubs. Scrapes are bare patches of pawed ground. Scrapes are always found underneath an overhanging branch or limb and these limbs are

Craig Smith examines a fresh scrape under an overhanging limb. Does that are ready to breed often visit scrapes. That's why breeding bucks can be ambushed as they check scrapes. A concentration of scrapes or scrape lines are the best places for an ambush.

frequently damaged by a rutting buck with his mouth or antlers.

Scrapes are often more important sign than rubs because does visit them when they are ready to breed and bucks frequently check their scrapes to find out if a receptive doe has been by. However, if you can find a rub line, a series of rubs made by the same buck that are strung out over a distance of a couple of hundred yards or more, you might also be on to something. A rub line marks a buck's course of travel. Posting along that line can pay off when the whitetail returns. It was scrapes, though, that led me to my first bow-bagged buck.

I was hunting a new area and the season was already open at the time, so I allowed myself a day for scouting to select a stand site. I found four scrapes. There were a pair of them along the edge of a stand of oak trees bordering a field and two more along the edge of a swamp bordering the oaks.

Transition zones, the border between two different cover types, are where scrapes frequently appear. Swamp edges seldom fail me when looking for scrapes and they are also good places to ambush whitetails, so I decided to take a stand overlooking the scrapes along the swamp. Since that location was furthest from the road and heavy cover was nearby, I figured bucks would feel comfortable visiting the area during shooting hours. The habitat was open where the other two scrapes were located, increasing the probability they were made under cover of darkness, and that's when they would most likely be revisited.

I decided on a stand in a tree about 20 yards downwind from the most promising scrapes. It's important not to take a stand too close to scrapes because bucks don't always go right up to them when checking for hot does. They often cruise by on the downwind side where they can smell the scent of any doe that has been there.

After making sure I would be able to find the spot I planned to hunt in predawn darkness, I left the woods. My good choice of a stand site was confirmed as I approached the spot to hunt the next morning. I jumped a group of five deer that were bedded within thirty yards of the tree I would be in.

I try to avoid disturbing whitetails when I take a stand, but that was impossible under the circumstances. In this case, I thought the animals probably weren't badly spooked because of the early hour, and I thought they would eventually start filtering back. The fact that a group of does were bedding nearby is probably why scrapes were in the vicinity.

Within 30 minutes, a whitetail materialized from the swamp and moved my way. It was a yearling buck with 3-point antlers and I put a broadhead through his lungs when he provided me with an easy 12-yard shot. Incidentally, I didn't use a tree stand on that hunt. I found a tree with a large limb I could stand on eight feet from the ground. That's where I was when I arrowed my first buck.

The stands I took both of my biggest bucks from were overlooking breeding areas and each location proved to be perennial producers. The spot in Saskatchewan where I dropped the non-typical 12-pointer with a Knight muzzleloader was located by guide Mike Aftanas. He found a valley in hilly terrain that was loaded with rubs and scrapes. He figured it would be a perfect place to ambush a buck.

When I first hunted the spot, I posted on the ground and took a mature 8-pointer. The following year, I returned to the same location, but waited in a tree stand. I got a trophy 10-pointer and another 8-point from that stand. Mike collected a trophy buck himself from the spot before I got the 12-pointer. Other bucks have been taken there since then.

The abundance of scrapes led me to the location in Michigan where I shot my best buck from the ground. Like the spot in Canada, the terrain was hilly and features of the terrain seemed to funnel whitetails there. After taking the trophy 11-pointer, I tagged an 8-pointer from the stand later in the season. The following year, I took a mature 8-pointer there and I hope in the future to ambush other whitetails in that breeding area.

I examine one of the larger scrapes at the breeding area where I shot the trophy 11-pointer from the ground.

As a general rule, the more time and effort that goes into selecting a stand for deer hunting, the better. This isn't always true though. Nor does a hunter have to remain in place for hours to qualify as a stand hunter. Impromptu, short-term efforts at ambushing whitetails also qualify and can be just as effective.

One fall when scouting a location for a spot to take a stand with bow and arrow, I was walking along a logging road when a doe suddenly dashed across it in front of me. The rut was on and I knew I hadn't spooked the doe, so I suspected a buck was chasing her. Realizing the buck might be close behind, I hurried to the downwind side of the doe's trail and hid among a clump of trees.

Fifteen minutes later, I heard the sound of another deer approaching and it proved to be a 6-point buck following the trail of the doe. The animal was so intent on trailing the doe, I was sure I was about to get a good shot at him. When he was almost to me, however, he temporarily lost the doe's trail and ended up on the downwind side of me. I tried a hasty shot as the buck turned to run after winding me, but my arrow was deflected.

That was one of my most hastily chosen ambush sites and one of my shortest waits for action. If I had only chosen a spot to wait a little further downwind, the outcome might have been different. At any rate, the experience still serves as an example of what to do if you see a doe during the rut that you think is being followed by a buck. Pick a spot downwind of the doe's trail and wait at least 15 minutes for a buck to come along.

Under those circumstances it's actually better to stay put for a solid 30 to 60 minutes because some bucks can be further behind does than that 6-point was. Also keep in mind that more than one buck can be following a doe, so don't give up if a buck goes by and you don't get a shot. Another one could come along. After missing the 6-point, I waited another 30 minutes on the chance he might return or another buck might come along, but I didn't see anything else. However, more patience might have been rewarded.

In good deer habitat, there are an endless number of ambush sites that can put hunters in good shooting positions for whitetails. Some stand sites are better than others, but it's not always possible to recognize these spots right away. All a hunter can do is make his or her best choice at the beginning of the hunt and be ready to change positions if necessary.

Old abandoned homesteads are another example of locations that can be excellent places to post for whitetails. It's not unusual for an old apple tree or two to be growing in such openings. The other types of plants and vegetation associated with clearings surrounding abandoned dwellings also provide food and cover for whitetails. In some

More than one buck may be trailing a hot doe, so be patient if you are posted along the route a doe used that's in heat. A pair of bucks are escorting this doe, hoping to breed her. Other bucks may follow.

cases, the former openings may be totally overgrown with brush and trees.

I hunted a tree stand next to an abandoned house in Alabama one year while hunting with Charles Dixon from Selma out of his Bow and Gun Camp. One feature of that homestead that attracted deer was a salt lick that developed from years of preserving meat with salt. The brine soaked into the ground creating the lick. I saw a number of antlerless deer from that stand. A few days earlier, another hunter had seen 8 and 10-point bucks from the stand. They got by him before he was able to get a shot. Dixon told me that plenty of bucks had been shot from the porch of the old house before the wood rotted enough that it was no longer safe to stand on.

I can't overemphasize the importance of scouting when it comes to stand site selection. It's the backbone of stand hunting success. The more scouting hunters do, the better. Maximize the amount of information about deer movements and preferred food sources in the hunting area by watching the animals and studying their sign before actually starting to hunt. This will make the selection of productive stand locations easier.

Keep in mind that deer movements and habits change throughout the fall and scouting should be a continual process to keep tabs on those changes. A change in deer movements often dictates a change in stand location, too, and may even require a change in areas, especially when hunting during late seasons in certain parts of the country. Whitetails in mountainous terrain and northern states are migratory, for example. Once winter sets in, deer move from mountains into valleys or from uplands to large lowland swamps referred to as yarding areas.

Continuing to hunt terrain that whitetails move out of during late seasons is obviously a mistake. Relocating to habitat where the animals start concentrating makes more sense. Posting along migration routes is also a good late season strategy.

Hunters who are as adaptable in selecting stand sites as whitetails are at avoiding hunters, are bound to do well. Keep an open mind and don't be afraid to try new spots. Best of luck in your efforts to select the best stand sites!

Deer & Deer Hunting Magazine *Editor Pat Durkin in a tree stand next to an old homestead in Alabama where many whitetails have been taken. Similar locations can make good stand sites.*

Chapter 3

When Tree Stands Don't Stack Up

The deer was only visible for a split second as it moved from left to right in an evergreen thicket. A noise had tipped me off to its presence. Unable to see the whitetail's head, I wasn't sure if it was a buck or doe, but I kept watching for another glimpse of the animal or others that might be with it.

Seconds later another deer appeared closer to me and the rack on its head was immediately obvious. The antlered whitetail was moving in the same direction as the first animal. Instinctively, I shouldered my rifle, holding it on the only opening the buck would pass through before going out of sight.

The whitetail soon appeared in the scope. When the crosshairs were on the shoulder area, I tightened my grip on the trigger. The deer went down instantly with a broken back and a quick follow-up shot finished him. That 4 1/2-year-old 9-pointer was one of many bucks I've taken over the years while hunting from the ground.

In that particular situation, the ground-based position gave me the best visibility. If I would have been in a tree stand, I doubt I would have seen that buck, much less tagged it. I was positioned just inside the edge of a thick band of evergreen trees that morning. The thicket was about 100 yards wide on the slope at the end of a ridge.

The evergreens gave way to a tag alder swale on the downhill side and a large stand of hardwood trees on the uphill side. I was posted near the uphill edge of the evergreens where I could see downhill into the thick cover and also watch a stretch of hardwoods on the same level. I knew deer traveled through both types of habitat. It was an advantage being able to watch both habitats, because it was impossible to know where a buck might appear.

By being on the ground, visibility into the thicket was best because there were fewer limbs, none in some cases, near the base of pine trees. That made it possible to see any deer that walked through the thicket within my field of vision, which was about 70 yards. Had I been in a tree stand, evergreen boughs would have limited visibility to about half that distance.

The stand site from which I shot the 9-pointer, as well as a number of other bucks. An uncle originally selected the spot. He also shot some whitetails from the location.

The year before I got that 9-pointer I bagged a 3 1/2-year-old 8-pointer from that same spot and I missed another rack buck the year before that. The site was selected as a hot spot for bucks by an uncle of mine (George). He shot some whitetails there before I started hunting the location, all from the ground.

There is another very important reason besides good visibility that my uncle and I hunted that spot from the ground every year. The location is in Michigan and it is illegal to hunt deer with firearms from tree stands. Based on the success of the state's gun deer hunters, it's obvious that it isn't necessary to hunt from tree stands to connect on whitetails.

Hundreds of thousands of Michigan hunters prove it every fall in one of the few states, if not the only one, where gun hunting from elevated stands is not permitted. During the past five years firearms hunters have bagged between 235,000 and 320,000 deer annually in the state. A record harvest of 357,000 was achieved during 1989.

Bowhunter Mitch Rompola of Traverse City with the mount of his best typical antlered buck arrowed from the ground, a 12-pointer scoring 181 7/8. He's collected plenty of other book bucks with bow and arrow while hunting from the ground.

Plenty of whitetails are shot by ground-based gun and bow hunters in states and provinces where tree stand hunting is legal, too, because there are other reasons for hunting from the ground than the fact it is required by law. As I've already pointed out, visibility is sometimes better from the ground than a tree. I do a lot of swamp hunting where evergreen trees are the dominant species present and I've found that, in most cases, I can see better from the ground than a tree and that's a definite advantage when hunting with a rifle, shotgun or handgun.

Hunting from the ground in swamps with bow and arrow can have its advantages, too. Mitch Rompola from Traverse City is one of Michigan's most successful bowhunters and he routinely hunts big bucks from the ground in swamps, even though bowhunting from tree stands is legal in the state. With archery equipment he has bagged an impressive collection of Pope and Young qualifying bucks from the ground— including a beautiful 12-pointer that qualifies for Boone and Crockett Records and currently ranks as the number one typical bow kill in state records maintained by Commemorative Bucks of Michigan. The antlers have an official score of 181 7/8.

The evergreen trees were primarily balsams and spruces where I shot the 9-pointer with a rifle. When hunting cedar swamps composed of mature trees, ground level visibility can be even better because cedar is a preferred winter food of whitetails and the animals frequently eat all of the leaves within reach. The resulting browse line makes it easier to see whitetails walking among the cedars.

When hunting among deciduous trees before leaves have fallen, visibility can also be better from the ground than an elevated position where hunters can look under the canopy created by the leaves rather than trying to look through them. During an early black powder hunt in Kentucky, being in a tree instead of on the ground may have cost me a chance at a rack buck. I was hunting with brothers Russ, Rick and Chris Markesbery, who make Rusty Duck gun care products.

The date was October 20th and most of the leaves were still on trees along the oak ridge where my hosts put me. Chris was posted along a creek at the base of the ridge not far away. About 6:00 p.m. I heard Chris

I check out the antlers of a Kentucky forkhorn I shot from a tree stand in October. Leaves that were still on the trees prevented me from seeing and perhaps getting a shot at a bigger buck that a hunting partner missed.

I shot this Montana 8-point with the help of Jimmy Dean on a cold, windy morning when it wasn't practical to hunt from a tree stand. The ice in my beard shows how cold it was.

shoot and got ready in case he missed the buck he shot at and it came my way. Not long afterward, a doe came running toward me from where Chris was and stopped 40 yards away, looking back from where she had come.

Then I saw the legs of another deer beyond the doe. Leaves on the trees blocked the whitetail's body and head from view. Seconds later a third deer trotted into view and I saw small antlers on its head. Assuming that was the deer Chris shot at, I lined up the sights of my modern muzzleloader on his shoulder when he stopped broadside and I fired. The forkhorn made a couple of bounds before going down.

I felt pretty good about collecting that buck until talking to Chris later. He had indeed missed the buck he shot at, but the whitetail he saw had a decent rack with at least 8 points. The legs of the deer I saw behind the doe were probably those of the rack buck Chris missed. Had I been on the ground, I'm sure I would have been able to see that whitetail and stood a good chance of being able to collect it.

I'm not complaining about bagging the forkhorn, mind you. I was pleased to score during Kentucky's first early season black powder hunt, considering the season was only two days long. However, given the choice between a forkhorn and 8-pointer, I would have preferred the larger buck. Under the circumstances, I was lucky that there were two bucks in the area and that I was able to get one of them. In most situations when a chance like that is missed at a buck, a second one seldom happens along so conveniently.

In some locations it isn't possible or convenient to hunt from an elevated stand due to the lack of suitable trees or the means to assume an elevated position. Hunting from the ground is the only choice in those cases. I've hunted terrain in Montana and Texas where there were either no trees or none large enough to climb and those aren't the only places where opportunities for tree stands are absent in whitetail country. Other times I've chosen to hunt from the ground even when suitable trees were present because I wanted to get in position quickly and quietly, no stand was available or I didn't want to carry one with me.

One fall when hunting in Montana with Jimmy Dean, for instance, he told me where to post on a cold, snowy morning while he tried to drive a deer toward me. There wasn't time to mess around with a stand, so I stood against an aspen tree on the ground and waited. I didn't have to wait long before Jimmy pushed a buck in front of me. It was a 2 1/2-year-old 8-point.

If I would have been hunting with bow and arrow, I would have stood behind the tree or other cover to help block from a deer's view the movement of coming to full draw. Concealment is more important for archers hunting from the ground than gun hunters because whitetails have to be closer before a shot is possible and more movement is associated with releasing an arrow than firing a rifle. Bowhunters who let deer get by them or wait until an animal's vision is blocked before trying to draw their bows have the best chance of going unnoticed.

Hunting from the ground can be more comfortable than hunting from a tree stand, especially when the weather is cold and an enclosed blind is utilized. The morning I shot that 8-pointer in Montana, the wind chill was below zero. Even if a tree stand had been present and in place for me to use that morning, I don't think I would have climbed into it due to the cold. An elevated position increases exposure to the wind.

More recently I did climb into a tree stand at the top of a Minnesota ridge on another cold, windy day, but I didn't last long. The cold wind cut through my heavy clothing as though I hardly had anything on. The wind also made my eyes water, making it difficult to see. On top of that, the wind was strong enough to rock the tree I was in. If I would have had a chance for a shot, aiming would have been difficult. It was easy to decide to take my chances on the ground that morning.

It's tough to beat the comfort of an enclosed ground blind when temperatures drop, but they can be comfortable in all kinds of weather and are popular among Michigan's army of gun hunters. Some bowhunters use

Enclosed plywood blinds like this one in Michigan are popular among firearm hunters because they are comfortable and they reduce the chances of hunters being seen. Some of them are stocked with heaters. Note the narrow windows, designed to reduce the chances deer will be able to see inside.

ground blinds, too. Homemade plywood shacks with sliding windows are commonly used. Some of the more sophisticated models have heaters to keep hunters warm regardless of how cold it gets.

Portable commercial ground blinds like the Super Blind made by Senco, Inc., P.O. Box 306, Marquette, MI 49855 are just as popular and comfortable as bulky homemade versions. The Super Blind weighs 16 pounds and the telescoping aluminum frame extends to a square shape measuring 56 inches per side. Ceiling height can be adjusted up to 6 feet, 10 inches. The blind's camouflage fabric fits tightly over the frame so there is no flapping to spook deer and will keep occupants dry on rainy days.

Besides comfort, the major benefit of enclosed ground blinds, is they reduce the odds that deer will detect hunters who are inside. It's possible to move without being seen by whitetails. Any sounds that hunters might make are also muffled. The chances of being smelled by deer may be reduced for hunters in enclosed blinds, but they aren't eliminated. Uncle George was hunting from a new shack during a recent

Some type of ear protection should be worn when hunting from an enclosed blind. Yankees third baseman Wade Boggs has ear plugs in place as he prepares for a shot from a blind.

hunt and was winded by whitetails approaching from downwind a number of times.

Wind direction should always be taken into account by ground-based hunters whether in a blind or simply standing against a tree. One possible exception is the Invisiblind designed by Mark Mueller, 3606 Central Ave., Catawissa, MO 63015 (314-257-2804). Due to this 17 pound blind's unique design, all human odors are supposed to remain inside.

Deer definitely can't see hunters who are inside the Invisiblind because there are no windows. You can see and shoot through the blind's specially designed front panel. Bowhunters are advised to shoot through the material with broadheads. Although bullets and slugs can also be fired through the material without affecting accuracy, Mueller recommends that gun hunters cut slits in the front panel to put barrels through before shooting at deer.

Extending gun barrels outside enclosed blinds before shots are fired is recommended to reduce ear damage. One fall George was hunting from a shack with his son Craig, who shot a buck with his rifle while keeping the muzzle inside the window. Both of their ears were ringing for days afterward. Some type of ear protection should be worn under those circumstances. Shooting windows should be padded to reduce the chances of making noise and to allow for a solid rest.

Situated against a large rock wall, the blind George and Craig were hunting from that day was, and is, in an ideal position for hunting from the ground. The prevailing wind direction blows in their faces and it is impossible for deer to approach from the rear, so they've never been winded there. The site has produced bucks every year George and Craig have used it.

Hunters who post in similar spots increase their odds of bagging deer from the ground. Setting up with obstacles (such as open water or a field) to deer activity on your downwind side is the key. The chances of being caught off guard, surprised and/or detected are reduced under those circumstances.

Ground-based hunters can also use the terrain to their advantage to end up hunting from an elevated position without climbing a tree. The opportunities for doing this are greatest in hilly, rocky terrain, of course. One of the first years I hunted with George, for example, he posted on a rock bluff that jutted out from a ridge. When at the edge of the bluff, he was 30 to 50 feet above any deer at the base of the bluff, which bordered a swamp.

There was a valley along one side of the bluff that funneled whitetails to and from the lowland swamp and the upland ridge. One evening George shot a spikehorn in that valley that was headed downhill toward the swamp. Although George was above the buck, he was still

I posted on top of this rock wall with bow and arrow in Kentucky to get a shot at an 8-pointer. The trail it was on is just to the right of the stump.

Blinds made of natural materials like this one are recommended on public property. Sides are usually high enough to block a hunter's body from view when seated, but low enough to allow full use of a person's eyesight and hearing.

hunting legally according to Michigan law because he was at ground level where he shot from.

I encountered a similar situation on a hunt in Kentucky while hunting with bow and arrow. The terrain was rocky and hilly there, too. I found a spot where a rock wall put me eight to 10 feet above a major deer trail. I stood next to a tree on top of the rock wall that I hung my bow in while waiting for deer to appear. A nice 8-pointer eventually showed up and I would have sworn I saw my arrow connect on him at 20 yards. However, when the deer didn't show any sign of being hit after I watched him move off, I realized my eyes had fooled me. I confirmed this by recovering my arrow.

Getting back to ground blinds, there are options other than homemade shacks and those produced commercially. Many gun hunters construct blinds from natural materials, such as fallen trees, stumps, limbs and evergreen boughs, available at or near the posting site. These are the types of blinds recommended for use on public property

George Smith and his son Craig look for whitetails from a natural ground blind with a plywood roof suspended in place with wire. Pieces of carpet under their feet help cushion them from the ground and eliminate the chances of their making noise when moving around.

owned by federal and state governments. Portable blinds that are removed when not in use are okay, too.

Natural blinds are generally built in a circular or rectangular shape with an opening in a convenient location. The sides should be high enough to block most of a hunter's body from view when seated, yet low enough so that it's easy to see and shoot over them. The advantage of these blinds over enclosed versions is it's possible to see and shoot at any angle. A hunter's hearing isn't impaired, either, like it sometimes can be in those that are enclosed.

A roof is optional. A cover can come in handy when it's raining or snowing. George suspended a piece of plywood over one of his blinds that was otherwise made of natural materials. Blinds built under evergreen trees that have lots of limbs take advantage of a natural umbrella effect provided by the canopy.

Camo netting can come in handy for converting natural cover into a blind. In some cases, enough natural cover may be available on the ground that it isn't necessary to modify anything. I've used a number of ready-made blinds consisting of blowdowns, stumps and clumps of trees growing close together. More often, I simply sit or stand against a large tree to break my outline.

All ground-based hunters should remain alert to increase their chances of spotting approaching deer as soon as possible. This is essential for hunters sitting in the open and it's also important for them to keep movements and noise to a minimum. Hunters who are adept at detecting incoming deer have the best chance of scoring.

I like to raise my rifle as soon as possible after an approaching deer is detected, to prepare for the shot. I make sure the whitetail won't see me move before doing so. Once the gun is up, I cover the animal until it's in the best position possible to shoot. By getting the gun up ahead of time, I don't have to worry about spooking the animal from unnecessary movement when it gets closer.

Another very important reason that some hunters choose to hunt from the ground rather than a tree is safety. They may be afraid of heights or concerned about falling from a tree. Unfortunately, too many hunters are injured in falls from trees every year. The opportunity for those types of injuries are eliminated when hunting on the ground.

Concern for hunter safety is one of the major reasons that gun deer hunters in Michigan are required to hunt from the ground. Even though hunting with firearms from tree stands is illegal in the state, some people break the law each year. A percentage of them injure or kill themselves in careless accidents. Department of Natural Resources officials feel that far more hunters would be injured in accidents if the practice were legalized and they might be right.

In addition to conventional ground level blinds and the use of natural cover, pit blinds are another option for ground-based hunters. Deer hunters can take a lesson from those who try for ducks and geese. If pit blinds help hunters connect on waterfowl in open fields, they can do the same for those interested in tagging whitetails. For that matter, they can provide an alternative in virtually any setting.

In some cases, a natural depression or hole can be found that will help hide hunters from deer. If one isn't already available, a pit can be dug when hunting on private property, once permission to do so has been obtained. Check local regulations before digging a pit blind on public property. When digging a pit blind, you should remove fresh soil from the area or cover it to prevent drawing attention to the location.

I've never hunted deer from a pit blind, but a friend of mine has. He reported taking bucks a number of years in a row from his underground hideout. The hole he hunted from was on the side of hill where the elevation provided good visibility.

Even though tree stands don't stack up for Michigan's gun hunters, those who hunt properly from the ground have just as good a chance of bagging a buck as hunters in trees. In some cases, they may have a better chance. Hunters who do have a choice between hunting from a tree stand or on the ground should consider factors such as visibility, comfort and safety, before deciding which is best.

Chapter 4

You Don't Need a Blind

Although there are obvious benefits of hunting from a blind when on the ground, it isn't necessary to do so to score. In fact, most of the whitetails I've shot from the ground, including that trophy 11-pointer mentioned throughout this book, were shot without the benefit of a blind. I prefer to use natural cover whenever possible because it's easier and requires little or no alteration of the hunting area. White-tails are intimately familiar with their surroundings. Something new, such as a blind, will be noticeable to them.

Deer that notice your blind will be on guard, and will have a better chance of detecting you. Some adult whitetails are so sensitive to disturbance of their environment that the presence of a blind will be enough to cause them to change their habits to avoid it. That won't happen when you use cover that's already there to prevent deer from seeing you.

In most cases, I simply sit or stand against a convenient tree trunk to break my outline. The tree serves as a back rest as well as cover. I normally sit on a cushion, folding stool or chair; I wear as much camouflage clothing as possible. It's important to be as comfortable as possible so movement and accompanying noises are minimized.

It's also easier to remain alert when you're comfortable. I rely on my eyes and ears to let me know when a whitetail is approaching, as most stand hunters do. And it is doubly

I prefer using natural cover when stand hunting from the ground. I often sit or stand next to a tree to break my outline, as shown here. Although I was watching a scrape line in front of me in this case, a buck eventually appeared behind me and to the left, and I got the 6-pointer.

important to detect an approaching deer as soon as possible when hunting from the ground, to increase the chances of connecting on whitetails.

One of the things I like most about posting in plain sight is I can use my hearing and eyesight to the fullest extent possible. It's sometimes difficult to hear sounds that deer make from the confines of an enclosed blind. When it comes to seeing deer from enclosed blinds, the walls impair a hunter's vision.

The hardwood tree I was standing next to when I shot that 11-pointer had a huge trunk that angled to the south. Most deer activity was to the north, south and east, but I occasionally saw whitetails to the west. I spent most of my time standing on the north and south sides of the tree where I could see and hear best.

When on the north side of the tree, I often leaned against the trunk. At times when I was on the south side of the tree, I often faced the trunk, looking around either side of the tree, or to the east. On sunny days, the shadow from the tree trunk provided extra cover and I tried to position myself to take advantage of that shadow. Shade or shadows can often reduce a hunter's chances of being spotted by a deer as much as real cover such as brush, limbs, leaves and trees.

The 11-point buck was traveling from south to north on the east side of the tree about 35 yards away and I didn't have any trouble getting the drop on him. The deer never knew I was there. I was on the north side of the tree when he appeared.

I shot two other bucks, both of which had 8 points, while posted by that same tree. One was to the east and was preoccupied with a doe and the other was approaching from the south. The buck coming from the south saw me, but I was ready to shoot when he did. However, the bullet missed. I think it was deflected by saplings, but I got the deer with a follow-up shot.

Evergreen trees often provide excellent natural cover for waiting out whitetails, too. In fact, they usually provide more cover than hardwood trees. Clumps of evergreens growing close together can work as a perfect natural blind. The same thing is true for some coniferous trees such as spruces, with limbs growing right to the ground.

One of the best natural blinds I've used was a large spruce. I was able to snuggle up next to the trunk between limbs without pruning any of them. The limbs were far enough apart that I had a clear view of areas that whitetails traveled through. Getting a bullet between the limbs was no problem, either. I was so well concealed that a deer or person would have had to be standing right next to the tree to see me. Even then, it would have been difficult.

Another spot that worked well for me consisted of a large aspen tree with balsam fir trees growing around it. The tree trunks were spaced far

Stumps can provide enough natural cover to make effective stand sites. I shot a number of bucks while sitting against a stump near a breeding area.

I drag the wide antlered 8-point, which was my first decent buck, that I shot while sitting next to a stump.

enough apart to allow good visibility, but were close enough to help screen me from view of nearby whitetails. I normally stood with my back against the aspen.

Over a three-year period, I shot at least two mature bucks from that spot and missed a third. My uncle started hunting there before me, and he also collected a number of bucks.

Fallen trees and stumps are also handy to sit against or on. I remember one particular stump where I sat during a number of gun deer seasons while filling buck tags. I shot my first respectable buck from that stump, a 3 1/2-year-old 8-pointer that barely scored 100. The beams were long and wide, but the tines were short and

This blowdown served as a natural blind one December while I was hunting with a muzzleloader. I shot a spikehorn from the spot.

A couple of large rubs on trees like this one being examined by Bill Jordan indicated a good buck was in the area. They helped me decide to use the stump as a stand site. My brother and I both shot other bucks from that stump during the years that followed.

uneven. Although his antlers did not score well, he was still a fine buck and I was elated to get him.

That stump overlooked a breeding area similar to the spot where I shot the big 11-pointer. There were a number of scrapes and rubs on an oval-shaped patch of upland about 10 acres in size that was surrounded by swamp. Most of the buck sign was concentrated near the east end of the upland and the stump was 30 to 40 yards from many of the scrapes. A couple of large trees had been rubbed by a buck with a decent rack and that's why I decided to sit there.

I got the 8-pointer on the evening of the second day of gun season and I'm sure he was the one making the big rubs. I shot at least four other bucks when sitting by that stump over a period of years. One was a smaller 8-pointer, a 6-pointer, a 3-pointer and a spikehorn.

One year my brother and I each shot a spikehorn from that stump, dropping them both in about the same place. I scored on opening morning and saw a number of other deer, one of which I think was another buck. Bruce didn't have much luck where he had been hunting on opening day, so he moved to the stump on the second day. Bruce scored during the afternoon. The spike my brother shot was sniffing the gut pile from my buck as Bruce pulled the trigger.

A fallen tree provided me with plenty of cover one December when I was hunting with a muzzleloader. The windfall was in a swamp close to a major runway leading into an active cutting where deer were feeding at night. Most importantly, the fallen tree was downwind from the trail. My head and shoulders were the only part of my anatomy visible above the horizontal tree trunk. Snow that had piled up under the tree also helped screen me from view of passing whitetails.

I saw a buck the first night, but the line of fire was too brushy for a shot. Things finally came together on the last day of the season. About 5:00 p.m. on December 12th a spikehorn trotted by no more than 15 yards away and with the iron-sighted rifle I put a round ball through his heart.

Another advantage of not using a blind when posting on the ground is you can set up to wait in a new area quickly and quietly. It's essential to settle down quickly when you find a spot that looks promising and there isn't much time to hunt. The day before Thanksgiving, 1994, Michigan hunter Lanny Higley from Fowlerville, for example, bagged a Boone and Crockett qualifying buck in a new spot by doing that very thing.

Walking along a logging road an uncle of his recommended, Higley found a patch of high ground that he liked surrounded by swamp. It was 5:00 p.m. at the time and there wasn't much more than 30 minutes of legal hunting time left in the day. He opened his folding seat and sat down where he had a good view of his surroundings. Twenty-five minutes later, a group of seven does appeared, soon followed by a trophy 12-point buck. The antlers had a gross score of 183 7/8 and netted 172

7/8 after 11 inches of deductions were subtracted.

Bowhunters can also score from the ground by using natural cover. My friend Jim Butler could have done so one December during the late season. He normally hunts from a tree stand, but on this particular evening he spent most of his time checking out a new area and by the time he decided on a well-used deer trail he wanted to watch, it was too late to put a tree stand up. So he selected a spot on the ground that provided plenty of cover and waited. The trail he had his eye on led to a feeding area.

Jim wasn't in position long when a doe walked by on the runway and he soon saw a second whitetail that was following her. It was a buck that looked like it had 8-point antlers. The doe had no idea Jim was there when she

Lanny Higley with the mount of a Boone and Crockett qualifying buck scoring 172 7/8 that he shot when selecting a spot to post late in the day.

walked by him, but the trail looped around downwind of him. Unfortunately, the doe smelled the archer before the buck was in position for a shot. She spooked the buck when she blew.

The doe appeared to be in heat, so Jim thought another buck might follow in her footsteps. To avoid the possibility of having the same thing happen again, he moved to the opposite side of the trail where the wind was more favorable. The bowhunter was still in the process of getting settled when a second buck came along trailing the hot doe.

The circumstances were ideal this time. The antlered whitetail stopped broadside about 15 feet away and then looked toward where Jim had originally been. He brought his recurve bow to full draw without the deer knowing he was there. This buck was smaller than the first one, though, only having four or six points, so Jim decided to pass him up. He got enough satisfaction out of knowing he could have killed that buck.

The move that Jim made after the doe winded him illustrates another advantage of using natural cover when hunting from the ground. He made the move quickly and easily, enabling him to be in position when the second buck came along a short time later. It would have been

Herb Miller with Boone and Crockett non-typical he shot from the ground with bow and arrow when using natural cover. He rattled and grunted the buck in. The antlers scored 196 7/8 and ranked as a Michigan state record among non-typical bow kills until 1996.

impossible to move a blind in the same amount of time. More disturbance would have been involved, too. As Jim did, I routinely shift positions when the wind changes to avoid being smelled by deer on hot runways, and other hunters would be wise to do the same.

If you are in a blind when the wind shifts directions, a hunter can move to natural cover to reduce the chances of being winded. It's not necessary to take the blind with you.

Herb Miller from Brooklyn, Michigan, scored from the ground with the aid of natural cover while bowhunting on November 8, 1993, arrowing a whitetail with a huge non-typical rack containing 22 points. Those antlers scored 196 7/8, setting a new state record among non-typical bow kills.

Herb had seen the trophy buck at least twice while hunting from tree stands, but something had prevented him from getting a shot each time. On November 8th he decided to try something different by hunting from the ground. He also decided to try rattling. The spot he selected to set up for rattling was in the open hardwoods. He positioned himself behind a big stump and propped one end of a log on the stump for added cover.

He had hit the artificial antlers together no more than two times when a spikehorn materialized practically on top of him and was gone before he could react. Herb grunted with his Woods Wise Mini-Tube in an effort to get the spike to come back, but the buck was long gone. If that yearling buck had given Miller a shot, he would have taken it. He had been hunting over a month at that point without getting a shot and he hadn't had a buck that close all season.

After five minutes, Herb went through another rattling sequence and then tried it a third time. While rattling, he turned to look behind him and spotted the big non-typical 150 to 200 yards away. The rattling obviously had the whitetail fired up because he was raking trees with his antlers and stomping the ground with his hooves.

Then the deer grunted and Herb grunted back. That brought the buck 50 yards closer before it stopped to look for what it thought was another deer. Concerned about being seen if he moved, Miller froze. When the whitetail looked away, he clicked the antlers together quickly and that had the desired effect. The dominant buck approached at a steady pace.

Herb put the antlers aside then, needing his hands to grip his bow. The grunt call was all he needed to keep the buck coming.

"He came in at a slow trot," Herb related. "He was coming right in and he'd grunt and I would grunt back. Every time he grunted back he sounded madder. The closer he got, the more aggravated he got because he couldn't see me. Then he really got mad!

"He was kinda zigzagging all over and he's looking for two bucks fighting and he's not seeing anything. He stopped and picked out a decent size sapling and rips it right out of the ground with his antlers. Saliva's coming out of his mouth and he's blowing stuff out of his nose. He's hot!

"Just about that time, he hits where that spikehorn came through," Miller continued. "Man, his old head drops down and he started coming closer. Evidently he thought the spikehorn was screwing with him.

"He got within about 40 yards and I wondered, 'What am I going to do?' I decided not to move. I didn't want to take a chance of spooking him before he was in position for a good shot. There was a tree in the shape of a Y between us. I decided to take my chance when he clears that tree because when he comes around that tree I haven't got any choice. He'll be right on top of me.

"When he was 25 feet away he was still walking with his head down and at a slight angle toward me. He was about 15 feet from me when he cleared the tree and I said, 'It isn't going to get any better,' and I just touched the trigger. I saw the arrow hit and I counted two ribs in front of it.

"The minute I hit him, he was literally gone. I waited about a half hour before I started looking around. I found blood eight feet high on a tree that must have been sprayed when he whirled to go. I did a dance at that point because I was one happy camper!"

The buck had a dressed weight of 211 pounds and was aged at 5 1/2 or 6 1/2.

Hunting from the ground without a blind doesn't get any better than that! There's a special satisfaction that comes from shooting a whitetail on its own turf, especially a big one, by taking advantage of its environment to pull off an ambush. There are normally a variety of natural features in whitetail country that can be used in place of a blind.

It's simply a matter of selecting those that work best for you. If one situation doesn't do the job, try another.

And don't limit your choice of setups to those mentioned here. Rocks, boulders and other natural features can also work. Manmade items that have become a part of the landscape might also serve as "natural" blinds. Some examples that come to mind are hay bales, abandoned cabins or homes and old car bodies or machinery.

There are plenty of old homesteads in deer country that haven't been used for years because they are no longer fit for occupancy. Some of these buildings are still standing and their windows have long since fallen out. Most of these structures are accepted by local deer as part of their habitat. Those that are safe to enter can be used as blinds. I know of at least two outhouses at old homesteads that served as blinds. I also know of abandoned homes in the middle of farm fields that bowhunters have successfully used as blinds to arrow whitetails.

Although there are plenty of advantages of using natural cover or features of the terrain as hiding places to wait for whitetails, there is at least one disadvantage. This applies primarily to situations where a hunter elects to go with a minimum of cover, simply sitting against the trunk of a hardwood tree or something similar. The key to success in those settings, as mentioned earlier, is seeing or hearing deer before they detect you and also preparing for a shot before that happens.

Hunters will obviously be easier to spot in the open than those concealed in a blind. Such a setup is probably not a good choice for those who are easily distracted or fidgety. Deer are great at spotting movement and hunters who can't keep still have a high risk of being seen.

Even hunters who can remain rock solid stationary for long periods of time can be at a disadvantage if a deer comes too close. If you're hunting for a buck, for example, and a doe

Outhouses like this one can serve as "natural blinds" at old homesteads. Abandoned homes that are safe to enter can also be used as blinds, too.

that's being followed by a buck practically bumps into you, you may miss a chance for a shot at the trailing whitetail by not being in a blind. It's important to avoid detection from deer you don't want to shoot in addition to those you do. One spooked whitetail can alert plenty of others.

When hunting locations with lots of deer and a high probability of being seen, it's obviously better to sit in a blind than against a tree in the open. Hunters will have to decide for themselves whether to hunt from a blind or to take advantage of natural cover and how much they want to be concealed from view, based on the current circumstances. When using a minimum of cover, it's important to keep movement to a minimum, too.

It's not necessary to remain motionless when you want to monitor your surroundings for moving deer. In most cases, that can be done by simply moving your head slowly. If you want to shift positions, stretch, or have something to eat, look all around carefully first to make sure the coast is clear before doing so. That will reduce the chances of being caught off guard. With experience, it will become easier to determine when to move and when not.

I've ambushed plenty of whitetails while using natural cover and I look forward to taking many more that way. It could work for you, too.

Chapter 5

Tree Stand Options

It's tough to beat a tree stand that's safe, comfortable, easy to get in and out of and, most importantly, is overlooking a big buck's turf. That description fits a Trax America ladder stand I hunted from in Georgia one fall. Host Bill Jordan, designer of the line of Realtree Camouflage Clothing, told me the stand had a reputation for producing big bucks. He said if I sat in it long enough, I had an excellent chance of seeing a wall-hanger.

He and videographer Chuck Jones reinforced the message by telling me about one of the bucks shot from the stand at the same time of the year the previous fall. The hunter was baseball star Wade Boggs.

I watch for whitetails from the ladder stand that I shot the Georgia 11-point buck from. Stands of this type are often the easiest to get in and out of, as well as being comfortable and safe.

I check out the trophy 11-pointer I shot from the ladder stand. The antlers had a typical 10-point frame with sticker points at the base of each beam, but only one of those points was over an inch long.

He got a beautiful 9-pointer that chased a doe around the stand several times before he could get the drop on it.

Chuck filmed the action and it's one of the sequences on a deer hunting video available from Spartan-Realtree Products. Even more important to me was the fact the 9-pointer was one of five bucks that were seen that day and it wasn't the biggest one they saw. That one got away.

I spent a lot of hours in that stand over the next couple of days, including one full day from daylight to dark, without any problems. The stand's comfort made the wait more bearable and the full railing/shooting rest enabled me to relax, knowing there was no way I could fall out, even if I dozed off. I saw deer during those two days, but they were all does and small bucks.

Chuck Jones enters the blind portion of the hydraulic stand made by New Heights, Inc., then elevates it by flipping a switch. He's ready to watch for whitetails when the blind is fully extended. There's a ladder that can be used to climb in and out of the blind in case there is a malfunction.

The buck I was waiting for finally showed up about 9:00 a.m. on the third morning. He's a beautiful 11-pointer and his head is now hanging on my wall. The antlers had a gross score of about 135, making him one of the better bucks I've bagged from a tree stand, but far from my best.

I've hunted deer from all types of commercial tree stands— climbers, nonclimbers (fixed position), ladders, tripods and even a hydraulic model—and they all have their place. The type of habitat you will be hunting in often dictates which type is best suited for your use. Self-supporting tripod or tower models, for example, are designed primarily for use in brushy or open habitat where there are no trees or the trees are unsuitable for stands. The hydraulic stand I mentioned is well suited for the same types of habitats.

Climbing, fixed position and ladder-type tree stands work anywhere there are trees. Climbers are at their best on straight-trunked trees with few limbs. Hang-on models are well adapted for use in limby trees, but either style can be used in most trees. Portability is another factor favoring climbing and nonclimbing stands because the lightest, easiest-to-carry tree stands fall in these categories. You will want to use one of these models, for instance, if you plan to walk a mile or more to reach your stand site.

What ladder stands lack in portability, they usually make up for in comfort, although some of the newer models are designed for backpacking like climbers and nonclimbers. The sturdiness of ladder stands and the ease of getting in and out of them increases their usefulness for big hunters. Ladder stands are often rated to support more weight than other types of stands.

You can count on that from Trax America's line of ladder stands such as their Penthouse and Griz-Bowmaster, because the man who designed them—Stewart "Bear" Dunn—is big. In fact, he

A rifle hunter in a Trax America tripod stand, which offers 360 degrees of coverage and a padded rifle rest. The stand can be modified for bowhunting by removing the rifle rest.

developed his own line of tree stands because there weren't any on the market in which he felt safe and secure. The Penthouse has a load capacity of 350 pounds and the Griz-Bowmaster has a capacity of 300 pounds. Dunn's original tree stand—The Griz—which is still popular, is rated at 500 pounds.

Due to the sturdiness and safety of ladder stands, at least one company—Apache Products—introduced a model designed for two people. It was developed primarily for the father or mother who wants to sit with their son or daughter to share a hunt, but it will work equally well for a hunter with a photographer filming over his or her shoulder. The "Dad-N-Me" stand has poly net seats and a weight capacity of 450 pounds. The child's seat has a safety belt and a gun rest with a camo skirt for concealment.

API Outdoors also offers a two-person model called the Grandstand to bring big and little hunters together. It is not a ladder stand, however, but a nonclimbing product with a rope and pulley hanging system. The Grandstand is rated at 350 pounds.

The hydraulic stand made by New Heights, Inc., comes equipped with a 40 x 42-inch box blind that is also roomy enough for two hunters. The unit has a lift capacity of 500 pounds and can be purchased with its own trailer or be mounted in the bed of any standard long bed pickup truck. Once inside the blind, you use a switch to lift it to an elevation of up to 20 feet.

This stand is the answer for handicapped or elderly hunters who would like to hunt from an elevation but are unable to climb conventional tree stands. It's the slickest stand I've ever used. On the evening I sat in the hydraulic stand, which was stationed along a wide powerline right of way, I saw two bucks chasing does. One was a forkhorn and the other had 5 or 6 points. I was looking for something bigger, so I just enjoyed the show.

Some of the roomiest tower (4-legged) stands can be obtained from Real Bark and Texas Hunter Companies. Both have elevated blinds big enough for two people. Real Bark manufactures circular blinds made of thermoplastic that measure 4 and 6 feet in diameter. The blinds come equipped with swivel seats and carpeted floors. Real Bark also offers a 3 1/2-foot diameter tower blind for "the economy minded, do-it-yourself hunter." It takes about 45 minutes to assemble the pieces, according to the company.

Texas Hunter offers wooden box blinds painted green that are over 6 feet in height and come in two sizes: 4 feet on a side or 4 x 8 feet. Sliding windows on both Texas Hunter and Real Bark blinds allow 360 degree shooting opportunities. Both companies also produce a variety of tripod stands that are smaller, lighter and cheaper than their tower mounted blinds.

Tripod stands are in the lineup of tree stands made by Trax America, Warren and Sweat and Strong Built, too. I hunted from a model made by Trax America that I liked. It had a swivel seat and padded rifle rest that made it possible to cover a 360 degree area while remaining seated. The stand can be modified for bowhunting by removal of the rifle rest. Standing archers can shoot over the bar, if left in place.

Getting back to ladder stands, new or improved models are available from Loggy Bayou, Amacker, Warren and Sweat, Loc-On and Rivers Edge. Loggy Bayou's ladder stands are 22 1/2 inches wide, 10 feet tall and weigh 20 pounds. Amacker's Adjuster Ladder can be secured to a tree from the ground, is 12 feet in height, weighs 31.4 pounds and has a weight limit of 300 pounds.

Warren and Sweat's Super Ocala, with a 12-foot height, is a taller version of the improved Ocala, which can be broken down into smaller 36-inch sections for lighter weight and easier backpacking. The company's 12-foot Spruce stand is adapted for use with a padded gun/arm rest.

Rivers Edge makes a Rapid Ladder, which is a folding climbing aid that can be used by itself or combined with any of the company's stands. Loc-On made it's Titan ladder stand safer by redesigning the seat and platform, adding ribbing to steps for better footing and adding a "ground hook-up system for greater strength and stability." The 10-foot unit weighs 20 pounds.

Pole stands are a variation of ladder stands. Instead of rungs,

A peg-equipped pole was used to provide access to a hang-on stand during an Ohio crossbow hunt. Poles are often quicker and easier to install than screw-in tree steps, and they don't cause any damage to trees.

I watch for whitetails from a portable climbing stand made by Summit. Note that I have my bow and arrows hanging where they are handy, and I have my hands in my pockets to keep them warm during a late season hunt. I bagged a yearling buck from this position.

poles are equipped with foot pegs for climbing. Pole stands are generally lighter and easier to carry than ladders.

Texas based Ambusher has three pole stand models—the Ambusher, Pole-Cat and Totem Pole. Using the company's V-Lok system, all three stands can be fastened to trees from the ground. The Pole-Cat comes with a gun rest and shoulder strap. A rest and camo blind are optional for the Ambusher. The Totem-Pole is the lightest of the models, making it most suited for deep woods use.

Amacker, API and Strong Built produce peg-equipped poles that can be used in conjunction with any hang-on stand. Standard height for all three is 12 feet, but extensions are also available.

The greatest variety and selection among tree stands is available in climbing and nonclimbing models. I prefer climbing stands because of their versatility. They are quick and easy to put up and take down and can be backpacked practically anywhere. On limby trees, they can be carried up and positioned where you want them just like nonclimbing models. Once in place, climbing stands that will remain in the same tree for a while can be accessed with tree steps to make the ascent and descent quicker and quieter.

I've used Summit's climbing stands for years and find them safe, sturdy, quiet, comfortable and easy to use. Older models come equipped with a seat and collapsible railing/shooting rest. Weighing in at 14 pounds, the Saber fills the requests of hunters who want something lighter. The climbing bar doubles as a seat and there's no railing on the stand. All Summit stands come equipped with safety belts.

One of the roomiest and most comfortable climbing tree stands I've hunted from is made by Trophy Whitetail Products of Townville, South Carolina. The deluxe combo stand can be adjusted for either bow or gun hunting and other models with fewer features are designed specifically for gun and bow hunting. All stands come equipped with safety belts.

These stands are designed for climbing while seated on a 3-inch padded cushion. Once in position, seats are adjustable to sit facing a tree or with your back to the trunk. The combo stand has a collapsible back/rifle rest that can be adjusted according to the hunter's preference. The most comprehensive set of directions I've seen for any stands come with those made by Trophy Whitetail Products.

I've had problems following the directions for assembly of some commercial tree stands. For this reason, I've found out that it is extremely important to do any assembly necessary on stands as soon as possible after they are obtained. If there are any questions or problems, the manufacturer can be contacted for advice. It's far better to find out if there are any difficulties with stands ahead of time rather than waiting until the day you want to use them.

One other situation I've encountered with at least one stand is missing parts. By putting a stand together soon after it's obtained, hunters should have time to get missing parts or replace the stand with one that is fully equipped. It doesn't hurt to try a new stand out either, even if hunting season isn't open at the time. Such preseason preparation can help you take best advantage of the limited hunting time you have once the season opens.

South Carolina native Brent Hunt, manufacturer of the Trophy Whitetail climbing stand, re-moves one of his stands from a tree in Kentucky after a successful hunt. These stands are one of the most comfortable climbing models I've used.

One fall I hunted from a Trophy Whitetail Combo Stand overlooking a Kentucky saddle that looked promising. One or more big bucks had stopped to rub their antlers on trees while traveling through the saddle. The buck I saw came from where I expected him to, giving me the shot I anticipated. The only problem was he only had spikes instead of a rack. The short time allotted for my hunt there was over before the one I wanted made an appearance.

Quality climbing tree stands are also available from Loggy Bayou, Amacker, Warren and Sweat, Buckshot, Trailhawk, API, Trax America and Lone Wolf. The Magnolia and Poplar are a couple of models made by Warren and Sweat. The Magnolia has a unique 3-tiered design. The seat and platform, complete with an adjustable railing/rifle rest, are joined together like many other stands. The third tier is a foot rest for climbing while seated on the platform facing the tree.

According to promotional literature about the stand, "You can sleep in it, stand anywhere on any edge or corner with both feet with no tipping, and it is very much like sitting in your easy chair at home."

Most climbing tree stands have weight limits of 250 pounds, but Amacker's Adjuster Chair Lounge has a capacity of 500 pounds. It's also heavier than most climbers, weighing in at just over 38 pounds, but this stand is "the next best thing to having a recliner strapped to the tree," according to the manufacturer. The Adjuster Junior, with a weight capacity of 200 pounds, is designed for light hunters and weighs 18.2 pounds.

Weighing 27 pounds, API's Alum-I-Lite Whopper has a weight capacity of 350 pounds. Amacker climbing stands have an adjustment feature that allows hunters to level platforms and seats to conform to a tree's taper. Once in position, an AM-Lock strap is attached to the stand to secure it in place. All Amacker stands come with safety belts.

Loggy Bayou's top of the line climber has a platform that measures 18 1/2 x 32 1/2 inches and weighs 10 1/2 pounds. A rubber-coated tree bar and a pair of rubber "tree teeth" on the back of the platform make this company's stands quiet while going up and down trees. The Master Hunter climbing stand has an adjustable gun rest that serves as a back rest while climbing. The platform on this stand measures 18 1/2 X 23 1/2 inches.

One disadvantage of climbing tree stands is they don't fit trees of all sizes. Most climbers are designed for trees measuring a minimum of 6 inches to a maximum of 18 inches in diameter, and that can vary depending upon make and model. Strap-on or hanging stands can often be secured in trees too large for climbers and, in some cases, trees that are too small.

Cost and weight are other areas for which nonclimbing platforms have an edge over climbing models. Hang-ons are generally the cheapest and lightest tree stands available. Loggy Bayou's Cheap Seat, for example, supposedly costs less to buy than it would to make it yourself. The folding seat and platform weigh six pounds and the stand measures 18 1/2 x 23 1/2 inches. The company's Master Hunter hang-on stand is 24 inches wide and a pound heavier.

Loc-On offers a fixed position model for "economy conscious archers" called Deer Crossing that comes unassembled. The steel grate platform with folding wood seat should only take 15 minutes for the average person to put together using "standard household tools."

Summit added a fixed position stand to their line called the Striker, which is modeled after the Saber, their popular climbing stand. Warren

Hang on stands like the one Steve Wunderlee is occupying in this photo are among the lightest, least costly and most popular models. The one he's using was made by Amacker. Steve arrowed a buck in Georgia from the stand.

and Sweat introduced Black Oak and Ash stands. The Ash is a deluxe version with a padded gun rest/comfort bar. Trax America and Amacker both have two hanging stands that vary in size.

Rivers Edge has two new fixed position stands, their Clearwater and Backwater models. Both platforms measure 16 x 24 inches, but the

Clearwater is made of aluminum and weighs 10 pounds. The Backwater is made from "expanded steel" and weighs 13 pounds.

Most tree stand manufacturers have a variety of accessories—such as tree steps, bags, pouches, bow and gun holders and more—adapted for use with their products. Many of these can come in handy, but one of the most useful, in my opinion, is an awning or umbrella to help keep you dry on rainy days. I used an awning made by Buck Pro from Wisner, Louisiana, on the day I got that 135 class 11-pointer while hunting out of Calloway Gardens at Pine Mountain, Georgia.

It was raining, so I carried the awning with me to the stand and installed it quickly and easily. All I had to do was screw a fitting into the tree above me. The canopy kept me dry and alert, so I was ready when the big buck appeared. Incidentally, Buck Pro also manufactures a pole type tree stand.

API offers an umbrella designed as a portable roof for tree stand hunting. Another umbrella for hunters called the Porta Roof Magnum offers 54 inches of canopy and can be obtained from Buck Wing Products in Allentown, Pennsylvania.

Commercial tree stand manufacturers often change the names of makes and models and add new features on an annual basis, so use the information in this chapter as a general guide to what's out there. Contact manufacturers for the latest information on their products. The *Equipment Annual* published every year by *Deer & Deer Hunting Magazine* is an excellent reference for what's new in deer hunting equipment. The addresses of manufacturers are normally listed in the annual. Also keep in mind that some models of tree stands are discontinued and some companies go out of business while new ones often join the market.

Chapter 6

How High to Go

What is the best height to hunt whitetails from when you are in an elevated stand?

There's no one answer that's always right. It can vary with the circumstances and the hunter. "Whatever you are comfortable with," is the response that is most often appropriate. Another good answer is, "Whatever works!"

I've shot my share of whitetails from tree stands. I was most often perched at heights varying from 10 to 15 feet above the ground when connecting. I was only 7 or 8 feet from the ground when I bagged a 3-pointer, my first buck with bow and arrow. That deer was 12 yards away when I released the fatal arrow. The animal didn't have a clue anyone was around.

I wasn't using a conventional tree stand when I shot that whitetail. I found a tree with a sturdy limb that was wide enough for me to stand on. That's where I was when the buck wandered by. The tree happened to

I grab my bow and arrows from the limb of the tree from where I shot my first bow-bagged buck. I was standing in the crotch where the large limb forks from the main trunk when I arrowed the whitetail. My feet were no more than 7 or 8 feet from the ground.

I was only seven or eight feet from the ground, standing on a convenient tree limb, when I took this 3-pointer. This was my first buck with bow and arrow.

be positioned within bow range of a couple of fresh scrapes. I located the promising deer sign first, then selected the tree to hunt from.

It would have been difficult to construct or place a ground blind in the open hardwoods that wouldn't have been obvious to local deer. By getting off the ground and above the whitetail's normal line of sight, I was able to go undetected. That's one of the primary advantages of hunting from elevated stands.

It's actually only necessary to get about six feet above the ground to be higher than the normal line of sight of most whitetails. Average whitetails stand about three feet high at the top of their backs, and they often walk with their heads lower. When alert with their heads held high, most whitetails have a line of vision that is seldom more than five feet from ground level. Hunters who are 10 to 15 feet off the ground are well above any whitetail's normal line of sight.

That position alone dramatically reduces a hunter's chances of being detected by deer. By taking advantage of whatever cover is available, wearing camouflage clothing (where legal), and being downwind from the animals, you have greater odds of going undetected by passing whitetails. Hunters who are elevated 10 to 15 feet above the ground, who keep movement and noise to a minimum when deer are in the vicinity, and who move to raise a rifle or draw a bow only when whitetails are distracted or their heads are behind trees, will seldom be pinpointed.

A survey conducted by *Deer & Deer Hunting Magazine* among its readers indicates that the majority of respondents perch 10 to 15 feet above the ground when hunting from tree stands. A total of 2,300 hunters took part in the survey and 57.5 percent of them reported waiting for whitetails at the 10 to 15-foot level. The most popular height was 13 to 15 feet, with 31.8 percent preferring that elevation. The 10 to 12-foot range was favored by 25.7 percent.

The 19 to 21 foot option came in third in popularity at 18.3 percent, and 11.3 percent of the hunters who took part in the survey said they usually occupy tree stands 16 to 18 feet high. Only 2 percent reported placing stands less than 10

Most deer hunters using tree stands climb no higher than 15 feet from the ground. That's usually high enough. Jim Haveman is shown going up an aspen tree with a portable climbing stand in this photo. When using a climbing stand, I usually tie a 15-foot length of rope to my gun or bow before starting up, so I can pull it up to me once in position. I can tell how high I've gone by the amount of rope that's used.

feet from the ground. A whopping 89 percent of the respondents go no higher than 20 feet when deer hunting from tree stands. Based on my experience and that of plenty of other hunters I've interviewed, it's seldom, if ever, necessary to climb more than 20 feet to be successful on whitetails.

The extra five feet of elevation between 15 and 20 feet will sometimes reduce the chances of a hunter being seen or smelled by a deer. The added height can also increase a hunter's view of the surroundings and may provide more shooting lanes. Hunters who climb higher than 20 feet ap-

By putting tree stands no higher than 15 feet from the ground, as guide Mike Aftanas from Saskatchewan is doing here, bowhunters have an excellent chance of making double lung hits, even on deer that are close to the tree.

parently want to maximize their visibility and eliminate the opportunity for whitetails to detect them in their stand.

Only 11.1 percent reported hunting higher than 20 feet on a regular basis in the *Deer & Deer Hunting* survey. The percent who said they positioned stands as high as 25 feet was 6.7; only 4.2 percent wait for whitetails at higher elevations.

I don't like to occupy a stand much more than 15 feet from the ground, especially when bowhunting, because I don't like to take shots at steep, downward angles. Those types of shots develop when deer come close to the hunter posted in a tree. When shooting almost straight down on a deer, you are likely to hit a lot of bone that can deflect or stop an arrow. And it's almost impossible to take out both lungs with a broadhead from such an angle, reducing the chances for a clean kill.

A whitetail can go a lot further with one good lung than it can when both are punctured. Adult bucks are especially tenacious. The further a deer travels from the spot where it's arrowed, the harder it is to recover. I've had enough experience trailing deer with both types of injuries to know the difference.

Double lung hits result in easy recovery. Wounds that damage one lung are another story. Unless a lot of blood vessels have also been severed, a whitetail can go a long ways after losing one lung. I know of some cases where deer have recuperated from injuries resulting in the loss of one lung. So if you bowhunt from high places, pick your shots carefully on deer close to your tree. As always, if you are unsure of making a killing shot, don't shoot.

I pause to admire the spikehorn I arrowed from a tree stand that was only 12 feet high. Even though the buck was only 10 yards away when I made the shot, I still was able to take out both lungs. That would not have been as likely from a higher position.

Shots at steep, downward angles don't pose the same problem for gun hunters as for bow hunters. Bullets and slugs aren't as easily deflected, and the shock these projectiles cause creates a lot more damage than broadheads. I wouldn't hesitate to take a shot with a rifle at a whitetail that is directly under my stand; but when bowhunting, I normally wait for a higher percentage shot. The nice thing about positioning stands 10 to 15 feet high when bowhunting is that it's usually possible to make a shot that can take out both lungs even on deer that are close to the tree.

Steve Wunderlee dropped this spikehorn instantly with a broken back. He's visible in the stand where he took the shot in the background. He was between 10 and 15 feet from the ground.

One fall while I was bowhunting oak woods in Georgia from a 12-foot high ladder stand, a spikehorn that was eating acorns fed to within 10 yards of me. I was getting ready to climb down when the buck appeared. I had already taken the arrow from my string, putting it in my bow quiver. By moving slowly and quietly, I was able to put the arrow back on the string and come to full draw without alerting the whitetail. I had a perfect shot at its vitals when it stopped broadside. The yearling whitetail went about 100 yards after being arrowed.

Steve Wunderlee from Illinois was hunting nearby that morning from a hang-on stand that was also about 12 feet high and he collected another spikehorn with a 12-yard shot. His broadhead hit higher than he planned, breaking the buck's spine, dropping it instantly.

When putting a stand in a tree that is in hilly country, you should consider how high you will be above whitetails that might appear on nearby hills and ridges. It's possible, for example, to be 10 to 15 feet from the ground in a tree growing from a valley floor, but below eye level of whitetails on a nearby ridge. If you want to be able to see deer on the ridge and reduce your chances of being seen by them, it's obviously important to be higher than the ridge line. It won't be necessary to climb as high to avoid detection when selecting a tree on the side of a slope or on top of a ridge.

The tree stand I shot the trophy 12-pointer from in Saskatchewan with a muzzleloader during 1993, for instance, was on a ridge in hilly country. The platform was 12 to 15 feet from the ground on the ridge, but at least 60 feet above any deer that traveled in the bottom of a nearby valley that the stand also overlooked. The ridge where the buck appeared on the opposite side of the valley rose up higher than the one I was on, but it was more than 100 yards away.

Due to the distance between ridges, I wasn't concerned about being seen by any whitetails on the far ridge. I was high enough to avoid being seen by any bucks on the same ridge as me. In fact, I had shot a pair of nice bucks on that ridge from a similar stand during previous hunts.

When the 12-pointer showed up, he was at my elevation. The fact that he was following a doe dramatically reduced the chances of him noticing the movement I made while raising my rifle. The appearance of the doe and her fawn ahead of the buck also helped prepare me for the shot. Even if the buck had not been distracted, I doubt he would have detected my presence, unless I would have made a loud noise to attract attention to myself.

Had I been hunting with bow and arrow instead of a rifle, I would have intentionally tried to attract the buck's attention by using a deer call or rattling. That would be the best means of luring the deer within bow range. Since the movement associated with rattling would have increased the odds of being spotted in that case, I would have tried to call the buck to me.

Because of the range limitation of bow and arrow, you should select stand sites to increase your chances of being within shooting distance of approaching whitetails. Positioning yourself within the desired distance of a well-used runway is one way of accomplishing that. That's what I did one November in Minnesota while hunting private farmland. I was posted in a permanent stand about 10 feet from the ground that overlooked a major deer trail leading to uncut corn on the top of a ridge.

I shot this Minnesota 7-point from a permanent stand that was 10 feet from the ground near a major trail leading to a cornfield. I shot the buck with the Knight MK85 muzzleloader that's leaning against the tree where the whitetail came to rest.

The stand was set up for both bow and gun hunting. It happened to be opening day of firearm season. Hunters were restricted to using shotguns and muzzleloaders in this area. I was using my Knight MK85 muzzleloader. I saw numerous antlerless deer throughout the day, but no bucks. When I finally glimpsed what I thought was an 8-pointer during the last minutes of daylight, I decided to take him.

The runway the whitetail was on led almost directly under the stand, but I wanted to drop him before he got that close, if possible. As soon as I saw the rack and made the decision to shoot, I shouldered the rifle and picked the deer up in the 2 x 7 power Bushnell scope mounted on it, watching for the right moment. The scope was set on 2x or 3x to increase my field of view.

About 25 yards away the trail the buck was on took a jog to one side. When the whitetail reached that point he turned his left shoulder toward me. That's when I fired, aiming for the center of the shoulder. My Knight muzzleloader was charged with 100 grains of Pyrodex and a saboted .44 caliber jacketed hollow point bullet.

The buck was knocked off his feet. He bounced back up again, but he only managed a few bounds downhill before his legs folded. He snowplowed for another 10 yards before coming to rest next to a sapling. The muzzleloader had done its job. The buck's antlers only had 7 points instead of 8, but I was satisfied nonetheless.

Had I been bowhunting, I would have taken the buck behind the shoulder with an arrow when he was 25 yards away. However, a better option would have been to let the whitetail go by me. Then I would have had a closer shot at the animal as it was angling away.

Different states have their own rules regarding the use of tree stands. Minnesota, for instance, has a law restricting the height of permanent tree stands to 16 feet. The elevation restriction does not apply to portable tree stands. Permanent tree stands are prohibited from some public lands in Minnesota, too. Permanent tree stands are illegal on all public property in Michigan. Be sure to check local regulations for restrictions on tree stands in your area.

Chapter 7

Tree Stand Safety

The worst scare I ever got while stand hunting for whitetails was when I fell out of a tree stand. I was in the process of climbing into the stand when the mishap occurred. After reaching the platform, I grabbed the seat, which I thought was securely chained to the tree, to pull myself onto the stand.

Unfortunately, the seat chain was loose. The chain had enough slack in it that it came undone when I grabbed it with my right hand. I had already transferred all of my weight to that hand. I was firmly gripping the detached seat as I fell away from the tree, crashing to the ground in a split second.

I'm glad the stand was only 10 feet from the ground, but a fall of that distance is enough to cause serious injury. Fortunately, I was not seriously hurt. I landed on my right side with my right arm under me. After my body hit the ground, my head hit an aspen tree, knocking my hat off.

Fortunately, I also had a guide, Mike Aftanas, with me. The mishap occurred seven miles from the nearest road in the Saskatchewan bush. If I had been injured, he could have provided assistance. As it was, the wind was simply knocked out of me. Mike endured a few anx-

I admire the trophy 10-pointer I shot from the Saskatchewan tree stand. Two days before, a chain holding a seat around the tree came loose in my hand when I grabbed it to pull me into the stand. I fell 10 feet, but, fortunately, I was not seriously injured.

Hunters who use permanent stands/steps made from wood should routinely check them on an annual basis for loose nails or rotting wood. Those problems, among others, have been responsible for lots of falls from tree stands.

ious minutes, however, not knowing if I was okay, as I rolled around on the ground gasping for air.

The guide asked if I was all right a couple of times, but it took a while to refill my lungs with air so I could talk. I ended up with some bruises and sore muscles, but was fine otherwise. What scared me the most was not only could I have been injured enough to bring my Canadian hunt to a halt, I could have hurt myself enough to affect my ability to deer hunt the rest of my life.

Mike's biggest concern was that my head had snapped back and hit the tree hard enough to injure me. Luckily, my body absorbed most of the shock from the fall. Had my head struck the tree first or if I had landed on my head, I might not have been so fortunate.

That fall really opened my eyes to the inherent dangers involved in hunting from tree stands and the importance of taking as many safety precautions as possible when doing so. I had been hunting from tree stands for many years without any problems and had become complacent. I now realize it's impossible to be too careful when hunting from any type of elevated stand. Always use the best equipment possible in terms of steps and stands and check them regularly to make sure they will continue to function properly from one year to the next. Most importantly, always wear a safety belt when in a tree stand. It's also a good idea to wear a belt when climbing in and out of a tree, if possible.

My story has a happy ending. I hunted from the stand in the tree I fell out of for the next two days, after Mike repositioned and secured the platform and seat. The first day in that stand I passed up a trophy 9-pointer that would have scored in the 140s. I wanted a buck with at least 10 points and I got him on the second day in the stand. The wide-antlered 10-pointer I shot had a symmetrical rack that netted 147 4/8 and grossed 151 1/8. The inside spread between the beams was 20 7/8 inches. I'm sure glad that fall didn't put me out of commission!

The fall also reinforced for me the importance of making sure, when climbing in and out of a stand, I have a solid grip with at least one hand and foot before transferring all of my weight to a new position. That precaution helped save me from another fall from a greater height the next year while bowhunting in Wisconsin. I was the guest of a hunter who let me use one of a number of tree stands he already had in place. The platform was 25 to 30 feet from the ground.

As I stepped on the last peg necessary to reach the stand, it broke. Thank goodness I still had a grip on the tree trunk with both of my arms when that step gave way. I hugged that tree harder than I have any other, as I slid a short distance down the trunk. Talk about a major scare! I climbed out of that tree as quick-

Some climbing stands may slip on smooth barked trees such as aspens, especially when they are wet or the bark is frozen.

ly as I could and spent the evening on the ground.

That step had been in place for a number of years and had obviously weakened over time. I think it is a major safety mistake to leave tree stands and steps in place from one year to the next, much less over a period of years. Continual exposure to weathering weakens and damages stands and steps. Cold weather combined with the flexing of a tree as it moves in the wind can crack metal tree steps. The next time they are used, they could break, causing a fall.

Constant weathering can also weaken straps and chains holding stands in place. My friend Jim Butler used heavy duty nylon rope to tie several tree stands in place on his property. He left the stands up all year. When he climbed into one of them a year after they had been installed, the "sturdy" rope broke. Jim managed to grab the tree, saving himself from a fall. Needless to say, he removed the weathered rope from the remaining stands.

Jim wasn't so lucky a number of years earlier while bowhunting for whitetails during December. The temperature was 10 below zero that evening, making tree limbs more brittle than normal. Jim said he took his time climbing out of the tree after dark, trying to avoid slipping on ice accumulated on limbs and steps. Nevertheless, one of the limbs he had been using as a step broke, and he fell almost 40 feet to the ground.

He broke his hip and a wrist during the fall and had to drag himself toward his vehicle. After a while, a friend came to see why Jim had not come home. He assisted in getting Jim to the hospital. The near-fall from the stand when the nylon rope broke brought back unpleasant memories.

Fortunately, Jim fully recovered from his injuries and he was back bowhunting from tree stands as soon as he could. Not all hunters who fall out of tree stands are as lucky as Jim and I were. Some end up permanently disabled. Others lose their lives.

The results of a valuable survey conducted by *Deer & Deer Hunting Magazine* about tree stand mishaps provides some insights into how

Always use a rope to raise and lower guns and bows from tree stands, as Bob Eastman of the Game Tracker Company is doing here. Make sure no rounds are in the chamber of fire-arms.

Always wear a safety belt when hunting from a tree stand as Sam Grissom is doing here in a homemade tree stand.

dangerous tree stand hunting can be. Of the 2,300 hunters who responded to the survey, 37.2 percent (855 individuals) reported falling from a tree stand at least once. Some respondents said they had fallen from elevated stands more than once.

According to those figures, hunters who routinely hunt from elevated stands run a significant risk of falling. The risks can obviously be reduced by being safety-conscious. One of the most important findings from the survey clearly shows that "...tree stand accidents can happen anywhere at any time to anyone under any circumstance." For these reasons, it is essential for hunters who leave the ground to be constantly vigilant about safety and the potential of falling.

Specific safety precautions will be mentioned later after more discussion about the survey results.

According to the survey the highest percentage of falls from tree stands happen when hunters are on elevated platforms (29.1 percent). A total of 28.8 percent of respondents were climbing a tree either to a stand or with a stand (to put it in place), when they fell. The percentage of hunters in the sample who fell while descending trees was slightly lower, but still significant, at 22.3 percent. Hunters who reported falls as they were entering or leaving an elevated stand amounted to 19.8 percent.

Structural failures of stands and steps, especially those that were wooden and homemade, accounted for the majority of falls. Older commercial tree stands made in the 1970s and early 1980s, as well as newer models that had been "modified" by hunters, were also prone to failures. Screw-in type tree steps commonly broke or pulled out when used improperly. Rotted wood on permanent stands frequently broke, or nails pulled out from them. Limbs being used as steps that broke were another common problem leading to falls.

After structural failures, slips and missed steps were the leading causes of falls. Rubber boots are especially slippery on wet wood or bark. Ice and snow also make climbing to or from a stand more treacherous. Some climbing stands are prone to slipping on smooth barked trees that are wet or icy, too.

Realtree Camouflage designer Bill Jordan from Columbus, Georgia, who I've had the pleasure of hunting with on numerous occasions, suffered serious injuries one year when the climbing stand he was using slipped on the wet trunk of a smooth-barked poplar tree. It was January at the time and he was hunting in Alabama with New York Yankees third baseman Wade Boggs. They rode a 4-wheeler into a swamp

If you don't have help when putting a ladder stand in place, be sure the legs are tied or fastened securely to the tree so it won't move when you are attaching the platform to the tree.

where Bill dropped Wade off first and then he continued on to another spot where he climbed the poplar tree.

After a while rain began pouring down and the water level in the swamp started to rise, so Bill figured he should get out of there. On the way down, the two-handled climbing bar slipped on the bark when the stand was away from the tree. After falling several feet, the climber suddenly gripped the tree. The force of downward motion pulled Bill's arms between the narrow handle bars on the climber. Having lost his grip on the climbing bar, his momentum pushed the platform his feet were on down further.

The platform finally stopped near the ground, throwing Jordan off of it. He ended up with his body on the ground and his feet still on the platform. It was an awkward position to be in, but Bill eventually managed to free his feet and drive himself on the 4-wheeler back to camp, a distance of more than five miles. It's a good thing he had the all-terrain vehicle with him.

Bill ended up with a broken collarbone, dislocated right shoulder and had seven stitches in his left hand between his thumb and forefinger from a cut he received during the fall. His neck and shoulder muscles were also damaged. It took him about 10 months before he was able to shoot a bow and arrow again. Deer hunters don't come any more experienced than Bill. If it can happen to him, it can happen to anyone, so be careful out there!

In the *Deer & Deer Hunting* survey, hunters who dozed off while in tree stands only accounted for four percent of falls. Those that lost their balance contributed to six percent.

The survey found out that the average distance of falls was 11.12 feet and that plenty of injuries occurred when falling that distance. Cuts and bruises were reported in 39.4 percent of the cases. Muscles and ligaments were strained or torn 25.5 percent of the time. Bones were broken 12.2 percent of the time. Permanent crippling was the result of 3 percent of the falls. Deaths from tree stand falls are thought to happen at close to the same rate, if not slightly higher.

Three percent may not seem like much, but when you consider approximately 9.5 million of North America's 11 million deer hunters spend time in elevated stands, close to 100,000 of them could end up disabled and another 100,000 dead after falling from stands. That's a sobering thought! *Deer & Deer Hunting* Editor Pat Durkin wrote three articles about the results of the magazine's survey, which have been combined into an informative booklet titled "Hunting From High Places." They can be ordered from the magazine for $6.00 per copy. The address is 700 E. State St., Iola, WI 54990-0001.

As mentioned earlier, hunters can save themselves from needless falls by being constantly aware of the potential and by taking precautions. Here are some safety tips to follow when hunting from elevated stands:

1. Never climb in or out of a stand with gun or bow. After you are in place, use a rope to pull them to you and, before you leave, lower them to the ground.

2. Always be sure your gun chamber is empty when raising or lowering it from a tree stand. Loaded guns held by hunters climbing in or out of tree stands have discharged, sometimes killing the hunter.

3. Always wear a sturdy safety belt when in a tree stand or positioning a hang-on stand. It's also a good idea to use one when climbing to and from a stand.

4. Inspect all equipment for cracks and weak spots *before* using them each time. Preseason or prehunt inspections of permanent stands and steps made of wood are essential.

5. Install tree steps properly, avoiding dead trees or rotten wood. Never leave steps in trees from one year to the next because the steps can crack or weaken in cold weather. The wood around the steps can also rot, causing them to pull out when you put your weight on them.

6. Do not leave portable tree stands in place from one year to the next.

7. Use enough tree steps to make getting in and out of stands easy and safe.

8. Be careful when using tree limbs as steps. Only select the sturdiest ones. Be aware that limbs can be more brittle and subject to breakage in cold weather.

9. When wearing rubber boots, be extra cautious climbing trees, especially when boots and steps are wet, muddy, snow covered or icy.

10. Avoid using climbing tree stands on smooth barked trees when the bark is wet or frozen.

11. If you don't have someone to help you fasten or unfasten ladder stands to trees, be sure to stabilize the ladder with ropes *before* you climb the ladder to prevent it from twisting or sliding away from the tree.

12. If you feel drowsy and think there's a chance you might fall asleep, return to the ground, your vehicle or camp for a nap. Don't try to nap in a tree stand.

13. If you are afraid of heights or feel unsafe or uncomfortable in a tree stand, don't force yourself to hunt from or remain in an elevated position. Under those circumstances, it can be impossible to relax and concentrate on your surroundings, which is an important part of deer hunting.

14. Don't hunt from tree stands when lightning moves into the area or on extremely windy days. Strong winds can make shooting from a tree stand difficult besides increasing the risk of tree breakage. One hunter in the *Deer & Deer Hunting* survey reported almost being hit by a dead tree that fell while he was hunting.

15. If you do fall while holding bow and arrows or a firearm, throw them away from you to prevent falling on them.

16. Make sure someone knows where you will be hunting (the exact location of your tree stand) and when you will return. When hunting with one or more partners, it helps to make plans to meet at a specified place at the end of the day. If someone fails to show up, he or she can be checked on as soon as possible.

17. No whitetail is worth risking injury to yourself. A fall from a tree stand may limit or eliminate future opportunities to hunt whitetails.

Chapter 8

Stand/Blind Preparation

Although one of the most important aspects of stand hunting is taken care of once you've found a spot (using either natural cover, a blind or tree stand) where you want to wait for whitetails, you are far from done in most cases. When it comes to consistently scoring on whitetails, little things can often make a big difference. Attention to details can

be important. Those details include making sure you and/or your blind/stand blend into the surroundings as much as possible to reduce the chances of alerting deer. It's also important to make sure you have removed all twigs, dead leaves and other debris that might be in the way when the moment of truth arrives.

Try to make sure you will be able to get a clear shot at whitetails that you see. Some pruning to open shooting lanes may be necessary. The best stand site won't do you much good if you can't easily find your way to and from it in the dark, as well as during hours of daylight. Based on personal experience, it can be much more difficult to navigate in familiar terrain after dark or before first light, so make sure you've got that covered. After having a hard time finding stands in the dark on a number of occasions, I've learned the value of marking trouble spots to avoid problems.

Having stands/blinds in place at least a week before you hunt will give deer a chance to get used to them. However, positioning them even a day before they will be used can be an advantage. I like to set portables up that are quick and easy to use just before I begin hunting, when possible. Bill Jordan and Joe Drake are attaching a ladder stand to a Georgia oak tree in this photo.

When to install your blind
or stand can be a consideration,
too. Where legal, you might
leave blinds or stands in place
for a while before hunting from
them, to give local whitetails
time to get used to them. A week
is usually enough time. In many
cases, however, it may not be
possible to place blinds and
stands until the day before they
will be used. That's normally
still an advantage because it's
possible to get in position
quickly and quietly, with a minimum of disturbance, the following day.

When using a portable blind
or stand that's quick and easy
to set up, I prefer putting it
where I want it when I arrive at
the location to hunt. If hunting
during the morning, I try to set
up before daylight. When hunt-

*Camouflaged blinds like the one Mark Mahal-
ic successfully hunted from are usually the
easiest to blend in with their surroundings.*

ing during the afternoon or evening, I get in position during midday
or early afternoon.

As mentioned earlier, some experienced whitetails will shy away
from a new blind or stand. Ground blinds are generally more disturbing
to deer than most tree stands, but ladder stands are more likely to be
noticed. By setting up just before you plan on hunting, you eliminate
tipping off some deer about where you will be. You also eliminate the
risk of them changing their travel patterns. By being there when a potentially spooky whitetail arrives on the scene, you may be able to get
an animal that might otherwise have been missed. The first time you
are in a blind or stand is often your best chance at a good buck that
might be in the area.

This is not always true though. I've hunted a number of stands two
days in a row before seeing the buck I wanted. By the same token, the
longer you hunt a given stand, the greater the chances that local deer
will start avoiding the area, especially if you've been seen or smelled
by some of them.

It's not usually a good idea to set up a tree stand for the first time
in the dark. The tree you plan on hunting from should have been selected and examined during hours of daylight when the location was

chosen as a stand site. If you consider it unsafe to put a stand in the tree you've decided to hunt from when it's dark, do it during daylight or the day before you plan on hunting.

Blinds should be positioned so they blend into their surroundings as much as possible. A bush, one or more trees or a boulder can help break up the outline of a blind. Blinds placed on the edge of tree lines often blend in well. It helps if the material they are made from is some type of camouflage. Even blinds made of natural materials can stick out like a sore thumb if they are not constructed where they blend with their surroundings. Camo netting is often enough to make a temporary blind from when staked between trees, but the material can also be used to help camouflage existing blinds.

Hunters are the least likely to be seen in blinds with only one window, like this one, because the interior is mostly black. However, the hunter's visibility is impaired. The best blinds have four windows that can be opened and closed as needed. Having at least two windows open is better than one. I prefer being able to see in all directions because it's not always possible to predict from which direction deer will come.

Although there are advantages to being able to see in all directions when hunting from an enclosed blind (which I prefer), having windows on all sides increases the opportunity for deer to see hunters moving inside. When bright light is shining in the opposite side of blinds from where deer are, for example, occupants can be silhouetted. This has happened to me on a number of occasions.

Blinds with only one window open on the front reduce the chances of hunters inside being seen because the interior is dark and they aren't backlit. These types of blinds work well in situations where most or all deer activity is expected in one direction and are popular among hunters watching feeding areas. The odds of being seen aren't much higher when two windows (such as the one in front and the other on one of the sides) are open. At times when light levels are low such as early and late in the day or when it's cloudy, the odds of a deer seeing a person inside a blind with all windows open are reduced.

Some of the best enclosed blinds I've hunted from have four windows that can be opened or closed as needed. If all windows are open, it's important to be more conscious of movements when deer are in sight than if one or two windows are open. After a blind is hunted for a while, it's often possible to determine which windows, if any, can remain closed.

When hunting from elevated blinds such as tripod stands, the opportunity for deer seeing inside are dramatically reduced, so having

Evergreen trees such as this white cedar Dave Bigelow is in here offer the best cover for hunters in tree stands.

Craig Smith reaches for the antlers of a 3-pointer he shot from a stand in an aspen tree. Limbs from balsam fir trees growing next to the aspen provided plenty of cover so deer couldn't see him.

all windows open at once is seldom a problem. It is difficult if not impossible to blend tripod stands in open habitat with their surroundings. Whitetails do get used to them after they are in position for a while, however.

Evergreen trees provide the best cover for tree stands and the hunters who occupy them. Be sure to select a tree with a trunk large enough for the stand you will be using. Some portable climbing stands won't fit around trees with large trunks. Evergreens normally have so many limbs that it's necessary to do some trimming to make room for a stand and hunter.

Hardwood trees with evergreens growing next to them are often good places to put tree stands, too. The overlapping evergreen boughs usually provide enough cover to screen hunters from view of whitetails. A cousin of mine named Craig shot a 3-point buck with bow and arrow from such a stand and he was so well hidden that it was impossible for deer to see him draw his bow.

In Craig's case, large balsam fir trees were growing on three sides of a large aspen. He put his climbing stand in the aspen and overlapping limbs from the balsams blocked him from view. Yet he could see well from where he was seated and he had an opening to shoot through.

Limby hardwood trees like some oaks, beeches and maples also provide plenty of cover for tree stand hunters. Hang-on type stands work best in these trees as well as in many evergreens. Oaks often retain a portion of their leaves after normal leaf fall, providing additional cover for the hunter.

Once you have a tree stand in place, you should draw an imaginary bow and arrow to find out if any limbs might be in the way— as does Brian Hoffart from Green Lake, Saskatchewan. Remove those limbs that might pose a problem. If you are hunting with a rifle, it's also a good idea to check for any limbs that might be in the way.

Even without the benefit of limbs and leaves, it's possible to successfully hunt whitetails from stands in hardwood trees. Deer seldom notice hunters 10 to 15 feet from the ground as long as the hunters are quiet and keep movement to a minimum, and as long as the wind is in the hunters' favor. I often try to position my stand in a clean-trunked tree on the opposite side of the tree from where I expect to see whitetails. The tree trunk then provides plenty of cover and it's usually possible to shoot around either side of the tree. Camo netting can be draped over limbs to provide cover in an otherwise open tree, too.

Once a tree stand is in place, check for any limbs that might obstruct the drawing of a bow or shouldering and swinging of a rifle by going through the motions with an imaginary weapon. Try this while both sitting down and standing up. If deer season is open at the time and you have a gun or bow with you, it's easier to check for any limbs that could cause a problem. Once you identify obstructions, remove them with a hand saw or pruning shears. Don't get carried away. Keep in mind that you want as much cover around you as possible. Before eliminating branches, weigh the benefits of cover versus problems that limbs may cause when a shot is offered.

When trimming limbs within easy reach of a tree stand, it's often a good idea to leave the sturdy stubs of one or two limbs that are at least five inches long each. They can be used as hand holds while climbing in and out of the stand, and they can double as hooks to hang a gun or bow from. I almost always carry a backpack with me into a tree stand and I hang it where it's handy yet out of my way while hunting. I always carry a pair of screw-in hooks with me for hanging backpack and gun or bow from, if no suitable limbs are available.

On the day I shot the non-typical 12-pointer in Saskatchewan I used a screw-in hook to hang my muzzleloader. The rifle was hanging from its sling when the doe and fawn ran into view. I grabbed it immediately, just in case the opportunity for a shot developed. It's a good thing I did, because when the buck came into sight moments later he stopped in an opening where I had my best shot. If the whitetail had made it through that opening before I was able to get the rifle off the hook, that deer could have gotten away.

When selecting a tree to hunt from, I normally consider the availability of natural shooting lanes. I choose a tree that will be downwind from most deer as well as one that provides maximum shooting opportunities. I don't like to do any more pruning than necessary. Major changes can modify deer movements. I've seen whitetails detour around wide shooting lanes that are totally cleared of brush.

Making sure you have clear shooting lanes is most important when hunting with bow and arrow because it doesn't take much of a twig to deflect an arrow. When setting a tree stand up, you should try to have a partner with you that can do the pruning while you direct him or her from the stand. If you are by yourself, take note of limbs that should be trimmed while on the platform and remove them when you return to the ground. Remember that the top of the back of most whitetails is no more than three feet from the ground, when deciding which branches to trim.

When hunting with a firearm, it's also important to have clear shooting lanes; however, it does not take much of an opening to put a bullet or slug through, so don't get too carried away. Concentrate on eliminating limbs that could block a clear shot or deflect a bullet aimed at whitetails that will be on trails in the vicinity. It isn't necessary to remove every limb and leaf between your tree and trails. When in a tree, you can shoot over a lot of brush that might block a shot from the ground.

Ground-based hunters will obviously have to do more clearing to provide open shots at deer using runways. Here again, it's important

A long handled saw like the one Debbie Knauer is using here can come in handy for pruning shooting lanes. Although it's important to remove limbs that can deflect an arrow, try not to eliminate any more cover than necessary to reduce the chances that deer will shy away from the area.

to remove no more than necessary to avoid alerting local deer, especially if you plan on hunting the spot soon afterward. It's not as critical if shooting lanes are cleared in the spring up to a week before hunting season opens.

Hunters who plan on using natural cover should clear away all of the dry leaves and dead twigs from the ground where they will be standing or sitting. These can simply be scraped aside with a foot. I always clear the ground to the left and right of where I plan on sitting so if I have to step in either direction to get a good look or shot at a deer, I can do so without making any noise.

When preparing the location where I shot the trophy 11-pointer scoring 148 4/8 in Michigan, I removed the leaves all the way around the base of the large hardwood tree next to me. That preparation allowed me to move all the way around the tree, without making any noise, while using the tree to break my outline. As it turned out, I shot the whitetail from where I was standing without a shift in position. On a number of other occasions I did feel the need to move around the tree to get a better look in the direction I heard a deer coming. In each case, it could have been another buck just as big, if not bigger.

Any limbs in the way of raising a rifle or drawing a bow should also be removed. The same goes for any branches that might make your wait uncomfortable. You don't want the stub of a limb poking you in the back while sitting against a tree. It's always best to get rid of possible distractions before you start hunting. If forced to deal with them while hunting, the extra movement or noise at the wrong moment could spook a deer.

From one day to the next dry leaves can accumulate at stand sites both on the ground and in trees. It's a good idea to make a practice of removing potential sources of noise, such as dry leaves, each time you hunt. I always try to brush snow off of tree stands before stepping on them, too, because compressed snow often turns into ice. Where snow is common, leaving a loose piece of carpet on the stand makes snow removal easy. The snow can simply be shaken from the piece of carpet.

Carpeting wooden platforms is a good idea anyway because the hard soles of some boots can make a lot of noise on wood when moving around. You don't want noise of any type to attract attention to you while shifting your feet into position for a shot at a nearby whitetail. Some tree stands, seats, chairs or stools have a tendency to squeak or creak as hunters shift their weight. Try to eliminate these noises by lubricating the joints, and by replacing nuts and/or bolts as necessary before hunting. If the sounds persist, it may be best to replace the item rather than risk spooking a deer.

Padded rifle rests can also eliminate potential noise at the moment of truth. Many commercial stands/blinds come with them attached. Adding carpeting or rubber to window sills is also a good idea. If nothing else is available, use a pair of gloves, hat or extra layer of clothing to pad a rifle before taking a shot from a limb or wooden window sill. Sand or bean bags make great rests for shooting from enclosed blinds, especially when trying long shots.

A lot of hunters who use tree stands leave a rope hanging from the stand to raise and lower guns or bows, which can be a good idea on private property. It's not as advisable on public land. The daily removal of portable stands is required on public property in some states, such as Wisconsin. I always carry an extra haul rope with me when hunting from tree stands, just in case someone has removed the one at my stand site.

Clothes pins with orange and reflective tape attached make great markers to insure you will be able to find your way to and from your blind/stand. Blaze marks on trees, surveyor's tape and Game Tracker line can also be used to mark a trail. Whatever you use, the markers should be removed when you are done hunting, if not before.

Some states also require hunters who leave tree stands or blinds on public land to have the owner's name and address on them. In that case, you should make sure your name and address are on the stand/blind before putting it in place.

When you are hunting close to a road or in country you are very familiar with, it may not be necessary to mark a trail to and from your stand/blind. But it's advisable to use at least some markers when in new territory or hunting a spot that's hard to find. Brightly colored surveyor's tape makes convenient markers, but the pieces can be hard to see in the dark if they are spaced too far apart. Blaze marks on trees are easier to see with a flashlight, but be sure to blaze both sides of trees, so the marks can be followed to and from a stand site.

Several types of commercial markers are now available that will glow when hit with a flashlight beam. These work well for finding your way to and from a stand site in the dark. A trick for marking trails I learned from Bill Jordan while hunting with him in Georgia was to use clothes pins to which both orange and reflective tape were attached, making them easy to see during both daylight and dark. Spools of white Game Tracker string provide a continuous trail to follow.

Unless you are on private land, you should avoid marking an obvious trail that other hunters might follow. Concentrate on only using markers at spots where you expect to have trouble finding your way. And don't forget to remove navigating aids when you're done hunting. It may actually be possible to remove markers before you're done hunting, once familiarity with the course has been established.

Always use a flashlight when going to and from stand sites early and late in the day, and especially in darkness. The lights not only make it easier to see, they let other hunters who might be in the area know where you are. Humans don't look anything like deer, but too many accidents have occurred under low light conditions to ignore the potential hazard of being mistaken for a whitetail.

Flashlights can come in handy to avoid snakes, too, in areas where they are found. When we were hunting in Texas last December, Bill Whitfield always reminded me to look for rattlesnakes in my ground blind. Blinds make perfect hiding places for snakes when the weather is warm. Most snakes will be hibernating when the weather is cold.

For bowhunting, brightly colored distance markers can be useful whether you are hunting from the ground or a tree. If you've got a Rangefinder, you can determine the distance to natural landmarks from your blind/stand while waiting for deer to show and use those as markers. Then when a whitetail does appear, you should be able to determine how far away it is without much difficulty. And if you've taken care of all of the other small details, the rest should be easy.

Chapter 9

The Well-Dressed Stand Hunter

A deer hunter's attire can make or break a hunt just as easily as the person's hunting and shooting skills can.

Consider the experience of an uncle of mine one morning during Michigan's gun season many years ago. It was late November and weather conditions were typical, with snow on the ground and temperatures in the 20s. While George waited for a whitetail, the cold worked its way through his inadequate clothing, thoroughly chilling him before noon.

George was shivering uncontrollably when a buck and doe made an appearance during late morning. He was shaking so badly he didn't even try a shot at the buck, convinced he would have missed—and he probably would have. In this case the buck only had spike antlers but the outcome probably would have been similar had that buck been wearing a record-book rack. There are any number of other ways a whitetail hunter's clothing can make or break a hunt.

Shivering hunters like George are more likely to miss a shot at a buck, if they are able to get one off, than the whitetail enthusiast who is properly insulated against the cold. Also, stand hunters who are dressed inadequately for cold conditions will not be able to remain in place long enough for the big buck that often comes later rather than sooner. And noisy fabrics have saved many a whitetails' life by warning the animals of danger as the hunters raised their guns or bows.

For these reasons and more, it is important for deer hunters to dress in such a way that they will be comfortable for as long as possible. Comfortable hunters are more effective hunters. In addition to providing comfort under prevailing weather conditions, deer hunting clothing should be quiet and should help the wearer blend into his or her surroundings. Fluorescent orange garments are required during gun deer seasons in many states and provinces, so hunters must keep regulations in mind, too, when dressing for a hunt.

Always check local regulations to find out what is required. Saskatchewan's clothing requirements during their firearms season, for example, are different than most other locations. A full suit of white, red or orange garments is required in addition to a red or orange hat.

The only orange I was wearing when I shot this 8-pointer from a nearby stand was on my hat. I was in Michigan at the time, which requires gun hunters to wear a minimum of a hat, vest or coat that is orange. I wore wool outer layers—a green and black checkered coat and green pants.

Research has shown that whitetails can see colors to some extent. Hunters who wear a full suit of orange will reduce the chances of being seen by deer if they hunt from blinds.

Most hunters wear white coveralls over their normal clothing. When snow is on the ground, as there often is, the white helps hunters blend in with their surroundings.

In regard to wearing orange or whatever bright colors are required by law, I recommend wearing the minimum specified by regulations when you are on stand. While the intent of regulations requiring the use of bright colored clothing is to make deer hunting safer by making hunters more visible to one another, orange garments also make hunters more visible to whitetails. In Michigan, for example, gun deer hunters must wear at least an orange hat, vest or coat to be legal. A vest meets the minimum requirements in many other states. I wear an orange hat while posting in Michigan, but I put on an orange vest when walking to and from stand sites. That's when it's most important for other hunters to be able to see me.

Veteran Michigan DNR Deer Researcher Lou Verme told me before he retired that, "Orange coats have saved the lives of more deer than hunters. We now know deer are not color blind. They see color in some form."

Orange sweaters, coats and pants that have splotches of other colors such as black or green aren't as glaring as clothing that is solid orange, and are better suited for use by deer hunters for that reason. Hunters who choose to wear a full suit of orange for safety's sake can minimize their visibility to whitetails by hunting from a good blind.

The key to being comfortable when deer hunting, regardless of prevailing weather conditions, is to dress in layers. Under the warmest of conditions, one layer of clothing, consisting of a light shirt and pair of pants or a one-piece jumpsuit, may suffice. As temperatures drop, layers can be added to provide insulation against the cold. A heavy coat or jacket can take the place of two or three layers of light clothing when temperatures become consistently cold. By dressing in layers, deer hunters can easily adjust their clothing throughout the day to remain comfortable as temperatures rise and fall or as their activity level increases or decreases.

Dressing in layers is the best way to stay comfortable while whitetail hunting in cold weather, as George Smith demonstrates here. He's wearing wool in this case and has an extra layer on the back of his chair. He's wearing Sorel boots and an orange hat, as required by Michigan law. Note the folded blanket under his feet that helps insulate them from the cold ground and eliminates noise.

Temperatures are frequently at their lowest point early in the morning and sometimes increase dramatically after a few hours of sunshine. You can remove a layer or two if you become too warm as temperatures rise. The same goes for the hunter who has been sitting for awhile, then shifts into a higher gear to track a wounded whitetail or perhaps to drag one out. Even though the temperature may not have changed, an increase in activity will increase the

Backpacks like the one this hunter has hanging next to him in his ladder stand are handy for carrying extra layers of clothing. To avoid overheating, you can carry heavy layers in a pack on the way to a stand. When the temperature rises during the course of a day, you can also store the layers you take off in the pack.

feeling of warmth and a layer or two may have to be shed to return to the comfort level.

Stand hunters who have to walk any distance to reach their destination should start out dressed as light as possible, carrying extra layers in a backpack. Warmer outer layers can then be put on once the stand is reached and circulation slows. This procedure reduces your chance of overheating and sweating on the way to a stand. Taking regular breaks along the way also helps.

Hunters who hope to sit for any length of time in cold weather should try to avoid sweating because this body moisture can accelerate chilling once you're in position. Sweat also increases body odor along with the odds that a whitetail might smell you. However, sweating is unavoidable under some circumstances. One way to avoid long hikes to stands is to camp nearby.

Smith's Law is to dress for the coldest temperature expected during the day or at least bring enough layers along to prepare for those conditions. Realizing that cold fronts can move in during the course of a day of hunting, I often carry an extra sweatshirt or sweater in my backpack. Hunters can always remove layers if they get too warm, but they can't add layers that they don't have. Each individual has different temperature tolerances. The amount of clothing it will take to keep hunters comfortable at various ranges can best be determined by trial and error. Remember that it will take more clothing to remain warm when sitting for hours at a time than when on the move much of the time.

I always wear long sleeve shirts when deer hunting, no matter how warm it gets. The long sleeves protect my arms from brush that would scratch unprotected skin while I'm walking to and from stand sites. Biting insects can be a problem when temperatures are warm, too, and covering as much skin as possible reduces my attractiveness to these blood-thirsty pests. I may even wear light cotton gloves when it's warm and mosquitoes are a problem, to discourage their interest in my anatomy.

Whatever types of clothing deer hunters wear, they should be made of soft, quiet fabrics—especially the outer layers. However, it is best if all layers fall in this category. A friend of mine was bowhunting one day, wearing a down vest with a noisy nylon shell under a soft acrylic sweater. He thought the sweater would effectively muffle any sound the vest might make. When an 8-point buck showed up and my friend started to draw down on it, the buck heard the vest move and he walked off before my friend could get a shot.

That's the last time he wore that vest, or any garment like it, when deer hunting. Down coats and vests are warm, but the vast majority of them are too noisy to qualify as good deer hunting clothing, unless hunting from an enclosed blind where no whitetails are expected closer than 50 yards.

Wool and Polar Tuff or fleece are the best clothing materials for deer hunting in cold weather. As well as being soft and quiet, wool retains warmth when wet. Polar Tuff garments have properties similar to wool and are water resistant. I find that one advantage of Polar Tuff over wool is that I can wear it next to my skin, whereas wool irritates my skin. When wearing wool, I normally have at least one layer of clothing between it and my skin. A disadvantage of Polar Tuff is that it sticks to the bark of some trees and makes noise when pulled away.

In terms of being soft, quiet and warm, acrylic sweaters are as good as wool. Thinsulate is another fabric that is both warm and quiet, according to friends who have worn it. Most of the sweatshirts, shirts and coveralls I've worn for hunting during early fall are made from some type of cotton blend material. Cotton and polyester blend garments are my choice for hunting in warm weather. Basically, any fabric that meets the criteria discussed above is suitable for stand hunting clothing.

There is a greater selection of camo patterns available today than ever before. They come in greens, browns, grays and whites to fit the time of year and surroundings hunters find themselves in. Choose the pattern or patterns that best fits the habitat you will be hunting in.

I've had excellent success with the variety of patterns available in Realtree camo. What I like about Realtree camo clothes, besides the fact patterns blend in with all of the settings I've hunted whitetails, is that pants, shirts and coats always have plenty of pockets for carrying accessories.

In this Saskatchewan tree stand Ned Meehan is dressed in layers that will keep him warm in temperatures as cold as 20 degrees below zero. He's wearing white coveralls as an outer layer, as required in that province. Be sure to check local regulations for any clothing color requirements.

I've also had no trouble locating garments made with this type of camouflage that are suitable for all kinds of weather conditions, from hot to cold to wet.

When buying outer layers for use during cold weather deer hunting, be sure to obtain coats and pants in large enough sizes so they will fit comfortably over all the other layers. Most of my wool or Polar Tuff clothing is at least one size larger than I would normally wear, to allow for multiple layers underneath. Under the coldest conditions when temperatures or wind chills are below zero, I will wear two pair of long underwear bottoms and a pair of jeans under wool or Polar Tuff pants. My upper body may be covered with one or two long underwear tops, a heavy shirt, a sweater and/or a sweatshirt and a warm coat. Occasionally I will wear a snowmobile suit made from acceptable material as an outer layer.

Ned Meehan from Westford, Vermont, has done a lot of cold weather whitetail hunting in Canada. He's come up with a layering system of clothing that allows him to stay comfortable on stand in temperatures as cold as 20 degrees below zero. I met him during a deer hunt in Saskatchewan and he shared with me his secrets for staying warm. He said he normally wears six layers of clothing on top and three layers on his lower body. The first layer on top and bottom is long underwear made of silk.

The other five layers he wears on his upper body are polypropylene and insulated long underwear tops, a Gore-Tex sweater, a down vest and insulated coveralls. He wears an insulated long underwear bottom and insulated coveralls over the silk layers on his lower body. Ned also wears what's called "turtle fur" around his neck, which is made of acrylic, and a polypropylene hood over his head. To help keep his hands warm he carries a Thinsulate muff with a hand warmer inside. He also wears heavy leather mittens (choppers) on his hands. He adds a set of white coveralls on top of the other layers, of course, as required by law in Saskatchewan.

When temperatures are in the 30 to 40 degree range, I normally only wear one set of long underwear and eliminate one or two layers on top. Even when temperatures are in the 50s, I normally wear a light set of long underwear because it's possible to get chilly after spending hours in a blind or tree stand without much movement. I've discovered over many years of stand hunting that as soon as the weather starts dropping below 60 degrees, long underwear is often the key to staying warm while waiting for whitetails.

Choice of long underwear is a matter of personal preference, but some of the newer materials are great for cold-weather use because they allow evaporation of perspiration from the body while keeping you warm. Polypropylene is good, but so is Capilene, which is what I've been wearing the last few years. Both materials are lightweight, warm and permit wicking of perspiration away from the body. I own a selection of light, medium and heavyweight long underwear that allows me to dress for any fall weather conditions—from cool to very cold.

Quality boots are as important for comfortable deer hunting as clothing. A hunter with cold or wet feet will feel cold even though his or her body may be adequately insulated. Insulated leather boots are a good choice for hunting in areas where the ground is generally dry and temperatures don't drop much below freezing. Leather boots are the only choice for deer hunting in areas with cactus, such as Texas.

Seamless rubber boots are best for hunting in wet areas. The insulated variety are recommended when temperatures dip into the 30s and 40s. Hip boots and chest waders may be called for in some cases. I've worn chest waders to cross rivers or marshes to reach otherwise inaccessible areas, then exchanged the waders for regular boots once on dry ground. A major advantage of rubber boots over leather is that they don't leave scent where you've walked.

Bean Boots, with their rubber bottoms and leather tops, are ideal for deer hunting in terrain that has a mixture of swamps and upland where water is no more than a few inches deep. Although developed in Maine, this style of boot is perfect for early fall use in the upper midwest and Canada, where I've done the bulk of my whitetail hunting. The Bean Boots I wear have removable insoles and a Thinsulate lining. I remove the insoles at the end of the day so they can air dry. The Thinsulate lining can be turned inside out to dry, too, if it gets wet.

Insulated Bean Boots are okay for hunting in temperatures that dip into the 20s, but the best cold weather boots I've used for stand hunting are of the Sorel and LaCrosse variety. They also have rubber bottoms and leather tops, but are larger and have more insulation than Bean Boots. Both LaCrosse and Sorel boots have liners that play a major role in keeping feet warm. I've worn a pair of LaCrosse Explorer

The rubber boots worn by Ronnie Groom in this photo are obviously the best choice of footwear for hunting in Alabama swamps as well as wet areas anywhere. An advantage of wearing rubber on your feet, besides keeping them dry, is they don't leave scent the way leather can.

boots the past couple of years. They've done a super job keeping my feet warm and dry in all kinds of conditions.

As with any type of boot that has a liner, it is important to take the liners out of the boots at the end of the day to allow them to dry. A spare pair of liners or boots is better yet to make sure you have a dry set to use for each day's hunt. Liners that aren't dry are less likely to keep your feet warm in cold weather. Dry socks are also important to keep feet warm during cold weather.

I was wearing the LaCrosse Explorer boots with one pair of heavy socks the day (October 28th) I shot with a muzzleloader the non-typical 12-pointer in Saskatchewan. The temperature was 18 degrees Fahren-

I wore a Polar Tuff coat in Realtree all purpose camo and a hat with the same pattern when I shot the trophy non-typical 12-pointer in Saskatchewan. There were four more layers under my coat. My pants were green wool, with two layers of long john bottoms under them. I wore LaCrosse Explorer boots, with one pair of heavy socks.

heit, with a significant wind chill. I was wearing two pair of long john tops and bottoms. One layer was heavyweight and the other was medium weight.

Three more layers were on my upper body. They included a heavy shirt, a sweatshirt and a Polar Tuff coat in Realtree all-purpose camo. I wore a pair of green wool pants over the long john bottoms and a camo hat. Although Saskatchewan law requires hunters to wear a full suit of red, orange or white and a red or orange hat during firearms season, full camo is allowed during the primitive weapons hunt, which includes bow and arrow and muzzleloader.

The weather was warmer on November 16th when I shot the Michigan 11-pointer from the ground. In fact, daytime temperatures were much warmer than normal, reaching the 60s and 70s. Mornings were cooler, but not cold.

I wore Sorel boots with two or three pair of heavy socks, one set of long underwear (lightweight), a shirt, a Polar Tuff coat and pants in Realtree Grey Leaf Pattern. I wore an orange hat at all times and added an orange vest while walking to and from my stand location.

Although most deer hunters wear boots, tennis shoes have their place during warm weather where the ground is dry. It's possible to walk quietly to and from ambush sites with these light shoes. Try to avoid wearing bright white sneakers, however, because they can draw undue attention from deer and other hunters.

Since an uncovered head radiates a lot of heat, it is important that the noggin be covered in cold weather. I normally wear either a Jones style hat or a pullover watchcap. I prefer a hat with a bill because it helps shade my eyes from the sun. When it's extremely cold and windy,

I will substitute a Polar Tuff hood or face mask to help keep me warm. Hooded sweatshirts can come in handy for keeping the head and ears warm when it's windy and cold, too. Hats or caps with porous coverings are the best choices in warm weather to keep pesky insects out of your hair and to help shade the face.

Headnets can come in handy for camouflaging your face and eliminating the glare from glasses. I prefer headnets with holes in them so visibility isn't impaired in poor light.

As far as gloves, try not to wear types that restrict gun or bow handling ability. My hands are usually covered with brown cotton gloves— I can feel my gun almost as good with these on as with bare hands. When bowhunting, I wear a golf glove on my right hand for drawing and releasing the string. My hands are put in my pockets to keep them as warm as possible when temperatures are cold. Using a muff as Ned Meehan does to keep hands warm, is also a good idea.

Any number of things can make or break a hunt for whitetails. Proper apparel that will keep you comfortable for as long as possible is at the top of the list. Knowing what to wear is as much a part of being a successful stand hunter as anything else.

Chapter 10

Guns, Bows, Bullets and Broadheads

What some stand hunters use to shoot whitetails might surprise you. A buck with one of the highest scoring sets of typical antlers taken in Michigan during the 1994 season, for example, was killed with a 64 grain bullet from a .223 caliber Model 70 Winchester rifle mounted with a 2-6 power Burris scope. The buck's 12-point antlers had a gross score of 183 7/8 and netted 172 7/8. The whitetail had a dressed weight of 175 pounds; the animal would have weighed at least 200 pounds in the round.

Lanny Higley from Fowlerville, Michigan, was the lucky hunter. The fact that all of Lanny's whitetail hunting had been done with a shotgun

Lanny Higley with the mount of a Boone and Crockett qualifying buck he shot in Michigan with a 64 grain bullet from a .223 caliber rifle. Although not the best choice in calibers for stand hunting, his rifle did the job. The .223 was the only centerfire rifle Higley owned at the time. Until the time he took the booner, all of his deer hunting had been done with a shotgun and slugs.

and slugs prior to the time he bagged the Boone and Crockett qualifier is part of the reason why he was using such a caliber when he got the chance to hunt in an area where centerfire rifles are legal for deer hunting. The .223 is the only centerfire rifle he owned. He bought it for woodchuck hunting and target shooting.

He shot the big buck at a distance of about 100 yards, putting the small bullet behind the deer's shoulder. He knew shot placement was critical, so he made sure he missed the heavy shoulder blade when taking aim. Although well hit, the whitetail ran 200 yards after being shot. There was no exit wound, so there was a poor blood trail. It took Lanny and his uncle an hour and half to find the fallen whitetail by following the blood.

Would you believe a 28-pound pull compound bow could account for a buck that was even bigger? It did for Linda Luna of Lennon, Michigan, during November of 1993. She used a Darton 20MX bow set at that draw weight to collect a 17-point non-typical with a dressed weight of 200 pounds. The antlers had a net score of 173 1/8, setting a state record among non-typical bow kills for women.

Linda knows the limitations of her equipment: 20 yards is the maximum range she takes a shot with

Linda Luna with the mount of a trophy buck that she bagged with the 28 pound pull bow she's holding. The whitetail proved to be a state record bow kill among women in Michigan. Linda has taken nine other deer with the same bow. (Photo by Linda Luna)

her bow and arrows at a whitetail. The big buck was 15 yards away when she nailed it with a 4-blade Wasp broadhead-tipped arrow. And the record-book buck was no fluke. Linda had been bowhunting for 20 years and took nine other whitetails while stand hunting with the same bow set at the same weight.

These two examples illustrate that taking a trophy whitetail doesn't necessarily require a large caliber gun with a big bullet or heavy draw weight bow shooting a fast arrow. Deer are fairly easy to kill, if bullets or broadheads are properly placed. Sharp broadheads are also more important than what draw weight bow they are propelled with, in terms of making clean kills.

Although they are obviously adequate for taking whitetails from stands, neither .223 caliber rifles nor 28 pound pull bows are the best choices for stand hunting. The same applies to .410 shotguns and .35 caliber muzzleloaders, despite the fact deer have also been killed with them. The best choices among guns and bows for stand hunting are those that produce the most consistent results (clean kills and good

Most of the whitetails I've shot while stand hunting with a centerfire rifle have been dropped with the Remington Model 700 .30-06 and 3-9 power scope laying on the ground in front of me with a nice 8-pointer.

blood trails) under a variety of conditions. There are plenty of options far better than those mentioned above.

Whether I'm using a rifle or shotgun, I like to know there's a high probability that the whitetail I decide to shoot will fall instantly when I squeeze the trigger. If the deer doesn't go down immediately, I want to feel confident the animal won't go more than 100 yards before tipping over—provided I made the shot like I should have, and there will be an easy-to-follow blood trail to lead me to the buck or doe. After almost 30 years of whitetail hunting, I've never been disappointed in my Remington Model 700 .30-06, with 180 or 150 grain pointed soft point bullets. I now prefer 150 over 180 grain bullets because of better per-

More whitetails may have been shot with .30-30s by stand hunters than with any other caliber. Matt Usitalo from Houghton, Michigan, proudly displays a Boone and Crockett buck he bagged with his .30-30 mounted with a 3-9 power scope. The white-tail's massive 10-point antlers had a final net score of 179 5/8.

Kevin Anderson used a .243, another popular caliber for stand hunting, to collect the beautiful 8-pointer he's posing with. The buck weighed 269 pounds in the round.

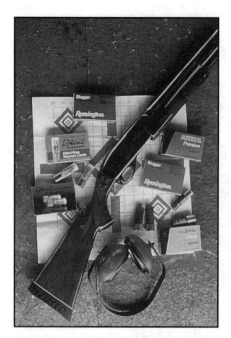

When it comes to stand hunting with a shotgun and slugs, the 12 gauge is the best choice. If you are hunting with a rifled barrel, use sabot slugs. Rifled slugs are designed for hunting with smooth bore barrels.

formance, but either will do the job. A high percentage of the whitetails I've shot with 150 grain bullets from my .30-06 have died instantly.

The 11-pointer that ranks as my best buck taken from the ground was one that didn't pile up on the spot. He was about 35 yards away and broadside, walking from right to left when I shot him, putting a 150 grain Remington bullet behind his shoulder. He took off in a death run like many whitetails do when fatally hit through the chest.

The deer barely made it 50 yards before going down. He was starting to lose his footing when I last saw him and I knew he couldn't go much further. The clatter of his large rack bouncing off of trees, followed by silence, verified that he had indeed expired. I found the buck just beyond where I last saw him during his death run.

There's a list of other rifle calibers besides the .30-06 that perform as well. They include the .308, .300 Savage, .270, .280, 7mm-08, 7mm Remington Magnum, .300 Winchester Magnum, .25-06, .243, 6mm and the venerable .30-30. The .243, 6mm and .30-30 have light recoil, making them ideal for women, boys and girls to use while stand hunting. I know plenty of men who choose to hunt whitetails with these calibers, too.

One hundred grain bullets are good choices out of .243 and 6mm rifles. If you're using a .25-06, go with 120 grain bullets. Owners of .270s swear by 130 grain bullets; 140s perform well out of 7mm-08s. Choices of bullet weights from 150 to 180 grains are available for the other calibers.

I prefer bolt action rifles because they are generally more accurate than semi-auto, pump and level action models. When I need a second shot, I seldom have difficulty working the bolt fast enough to get one in the chamber. In fact, chambering a second round comes automatically. However, faster second and third shots are obviously possible with a semi-auto rather than a bolt, pump or lever. There's no need to lower the gun from your shoulder to work the action.

Personal preference has a lot to do with action selection. Some hunters like the looks or feel of one over the others, and so that's what they decide to use. The type of gun a beginning hunter's father, uncle or friend uses is often what the novice selects, both in terms of action and caliber. A recommendation from an experienced hunter is normally all it takes to sway a newcomer's decision about what constitutes the right firearm for them.

Rifled shotgun barrels when used in combination with the new generation of sabot slugs have taken the place of smooth bores as the most accurate for whitetail hunting. Traditional rifled slugs are the top choice for stand hunters carrying smooth bore shotguns. I've had the best results in terms of consistent accuracy with Brenneke slugs. However, it's best to try different brands of slugs to determine which performs the best out of your gun. This is true for both rifled and smooth bore shotgun barrels.

Buckshot has limited applications for stand hunting, but these loads might be the best choice when you are posted in tight quarters where whitetails are on the move. While shotgun barrels with improved cylinder chokes produce the best accuracy with slugs, full chokes give better results when shooting buckshot. Even then, buckshot has a limited effective range of about 50 yards. The largest buckshot pellets are 00 and 000, but loads of number one and three buckshot have far more pellets, increasing the chances for clean kills at reasonable ranges. Pattern different loads at various distances from your shotgun to determine which ones give the best results, if you plan on hunting with buckshot.

Twelve gauge shotguns chambered for three inch shells are the most popular for stand hunting. Either 2 3/4-inch or 3-inch loads can be used in these guns. However, be sure to sight your gun in with the shells you plan on using. That's always true regardless of what type of gun you plan on carrying to your blind or stand.

If you don't like the weight and/or recoil of a 12 gauge shotgun, consider using a 20 gauge with a 3-inch chamber.

When it comes to shotguns, I prefer pump actions because I used them for years in small game hunting, before I started hunting big game. The first whitetails I ever killed were shot with a pump action Marlin 12 gauge with a bead front sight. Years later, I shot two others with a Remington Model 870 pump fitted with a slug barrel and iron sights.

I seldom hunt with iron sights anymore, unless I don't have a choice. Scopes are my sights of choice on centerfire rifles, shotguns, muzzleloaders and handguns. I like 3-9 power scopes on centerfire rifles and have a 2-7 power model on my muzzleloader. Low powered variables are also well suited for shotguns. Low power scopes with fixed magnification are great on handguns, but variables will work, too.

I've had good luck with Bushnell, Nikon and Pentax scopes. I really like a Light Seeker Pentax I currently have mounted on my .30-06.

Scopes are much easier to aim with than iron sights because the cross hairs and target are in focus on one plane of view. When using iron sights, your eyes have to try to focus on three planes of view at the same time—front and rear sights in addition to your target—which can sometimes be difficult, especially under low light conditions. The light-gathering ability of scopes are major advantages for shooting early and

I shot this 2 1/2-year-old 8-pointer with a Brenneke slug out of a 12 gauge Remington Model 870 pump gun.

late in the day. The magnification that scopes provide also give the stand hunter a better view of an animal he or she intends to shoot, increasing the chances of seeing branches that might interfere with a shot, in some cases.

All of the whitetails I've taken from stands with muzzleloaders have been collected with .50 caliber rifles, with good results. Front loaders in .54 caliber are also a good choice. I've found both Knight and Thompson/Center rifles to be quality products. Modern muzzleloaders like the Knights, with in-line ignition systems and double safeties, produce the best accuracy and performance with saboted pistol bullets. These rifles are also easy to disassemble for cleaning and to correct any problems that may develop.

Either .44 or .45 caliber bullets work well out of the Knights. Green sabots are designed for use with .44s and black sabots fit the .45s. I shot my trophy Saskatchewan 12-pointer with a Hornady 240 grain semi-jacketed hollow point bullet in 44 caliber. It performed beautifully. If you pre-

Saboted pistol bullets like the one being started in the bore of a Knight muzzleloader, as shown here, provide the best performance in terms of accuracy and clean kills from front loading rifles.

fer .45 caliber bullets, as veteran black powder hunter Toby Bridges does, they are available in a weight of 250 grains.

Regulations in some states may limit hunters to the use of round balls during special muzzleloading deer seasons. Be sure to become familiar with local regulations dealing with front loaders before hunting deer with them. In Pennsylvania, for example, black powder hunters can't even use percussion cap rifles during the state's primitive weapons hunt. Flintlock rifles are the only type permitted there. Percussion cap models are definitely the best

Tony Knight shows off a record book whitetail he shot in Nebraska with the .50 caliber muzzleloader he designed (resting on the tree trunk to his right).

Red Friedrich with a trophy non-typical whitetail he shot from a ground blind with a Thompson/Center Scout muzzleloader in .50 caliber. The rifle was loaded with a round ball.

for stand hunting. There are generally no restrictions on their use during regular gun seasons.

As a general rule of thumb, powder charges for deer hunting with muzzleloaders are determined by doubling the caliber. I've always had excellent results using 100 grains of FFg black powder or Pyrodex, by volume, in .50 caliber rifles. Ninety grains of powder sometimes produces more consistent accuracy out of some front loaders. A standard charge for hunting with a .54 caliber rifle would be 110 grains of powder.

Handguns are the only type of firearm with which I have not taken a whitetail. One year, however, I tried carrying a .44 magnum Ruger Blackhawk revolver. I practiced all summer with the sidearm, but managed to

Mark Janousek and the scoped .44 magnum handgun he shot his Boone and Crockett non-typical with while stand hunting. The 25 point antlers scored 203 7/8. When Mark couldn't find his ear plugs, he stuck .44 shells in his ears before taking the shot. (Photo by Mark Janousek)

miss two bucks with it during a day of hunting. The first was a spikehorn and the second was a trophy 10-pointer that ran by 35 yards away.

The .44 magnum handgun has always been the best choice among revolvers for whitetail hunting, using 240 grain semi-jacketed hollow point bullets. I've interviewed a number of stand hunters who have been successful with them, including one who took a buck with a Boone and Crockett non-typical rack. Mark Janousek of Olivet, Michigan, nailed an impressive 25-pointer while hunting from a blind in Eaton County about 5:10 p.m. on November 22nd one year.

Janousek used a Dan Wesson .44 magnum revolver with a 10-inch barrel. The revolver was mounted with a two power scope. Mark handloaded the handgun with 300 grain XTP Hornady hollow point bullets.

Antlers from the buck Mark shot with his revolver scored 203 7/8. Mark's book buck was 4 1/2 years old and had a dressed weight of 158 pounds. The B&C buck was the seventh deer he had taken with his revolver, although his first experience with the handgun was similar to mine. He missed a nice 8-pointer with the gun the first year he hunted with it. Janousek didn't hunt with the revolver for the next couple of years, but he continued practicing with the revolver to improve his accuracy. He was obviously better prepared when he resumed hunting with the .44 magnum because he hadn't missed with it since.

"I really like hunting with a handgun," Mark said. "It's more accurate than my shotgun, if I have a rest. I shoot 3 1/2-inch groups at 100 yards with it, but when hunting I like to keep shots under 60 yards."

Mark said he normally hunts from a blind and frequently uses the blind's window sill as a rest for his scoped handgun. Due to the loud noise his gun makes when he shoots, he always carries ear plugs in his pockets and puts the foam rubber plugs in his ears before taking a shot at a deer. The plugs reduce the chances he will flinch in antic-ipation of the loud bang.

Mark's booner was the second buck he got with his handgun during that year. At 8:15 a.m. on opening day of gun season, Mark bagged a nice 8-pointer with a 15 yard shot. The antlers had a 17 1/2-inch outside spread and he guessed the rack would score about 110. He had taken another buck or two with similar antlers.

On the 22nd Janousek moved to another blind along the edge of a wet swamp. On a road near the swamp earlier in the fall his father had seen a tremendous buck in the headlights of his car. As it turned out, Mark got the buck his father had seen. The deer was 70 yards away when he first saw it. The whitetail was walking through water toward high ground at the edge of the swamp.

As the buck approached, Mark got excited, which is understandable under the circumstances. He fumbled around in his pockets for his ear plugs and couldn't find them. Rather than spend more time looking for the plugs, he substituted a pair of .44 shells and had them sticking out of his ears when the buck stopped angling toward him at 23 paces. The whitetail wheeled and ran at the shot, but only made it 70 or 80 yards before going down.

Although less popular than .44s, .41 magnum revolvers offer an option for stand hunters interested in these types of handguns. Bullets for the .41s are available in 210 grain weight. Plenty of whitetails have been shot with .357 magnum revolvers, but this caliber is considered on the light side for consistent results.

Single shot handguns like the Thompson/Center Contender may be more popular than revolvers among stand hunters today. There are certainly more big game calibers available for the one shot sidearms, which have interchangeable barrels. Jim Jensen of Marquette, Michigan, has taken several bucks with his Contender from a blind—the biggest of which is a trophy 12-pointer that had a final net score of 164 6/8 as a non-typical.

Jim Jensen with the head mount of a trophy buck he got with a single shot Thompson/Center handgun from a blind. Barrels for this gun are available in a variety of calibers suitable for deer hunting.

Larry Weishuhn with a Georgia 9-pointer he scored on with a .309 JDJ caliber barrel made by SSK Industries.

On November 28th Jensen shot the big buck with a 75 grain hollow point bullet from the chamber of a .256 magnum barrel. At first the buck was facing him 60 yards away. Not wanting to take that shot with the light bullet, Jensen waited for the whitetail to turn broadside. When it did, he put the bullet through its lungs.

Jensen's handgun was mounted with a 1 1/2 power scope. He shot a 9-pointer scoring 101 with the same barrel a number of years earlier. That buck was dropped instantly at a distance of 20 yards with a neck shot. Another time, the avid hunter shot an 8-pointer with a 7 x 30 caliber barrel on the same gun.

Other calibers available in the Contender that would be good for stand hunting are the .30-30, .35, .44, .41 and .309 JDJ. I shared a Georgia hunt with whitetail expert Larry Weishuhn one fall, and he used a single shot .309 JDJ to collect a nice buck. The 14-inch barrel was made by SSK Industries and is mounted with a 2.5-7 power Simmons scope. He shoots 150 grain Nosler Ballistic Tip bullets through the handgun.

Magnum Research from Minneapolis, Minnesota, makes another single shot handgun called the Lone Eagle that is available in .308, 7mm-08 and .358 calibers. The same company makes semi-automatic handguns for deer hunting in a Desert Eagle model. The two best caliber Desert Eagles are .44 magnums. According to a spokesman for the company, their .50 caliber handguns provide 60 percent more foot pounds of energy than .44 magnums with 325 to 350 grain bullets.

The first whitetails I collected with bow and arrow were taken with a 42 pound pull recurve. I upgraded to a 52-pounder and hunted successfully with that for a number of years before getting my first compound bow. I've had good luck while stand hunting for whitetails with

Chris Markesbery walks up on a Kentucky 6-pointer he arrowed from a tree stand with a compound bow. Bows with a draw weight of at least 40 pounds have plenty of power for bagging whitetails. Compounds make it easier to shoot draw weights up to 70 pounds for flatter arrow trajectory and speed.

compounds made by Bear, Golden Eagle, PSE and Darton, having draw weights that varied from 50 to 60 pounds.

There are plenty of quality bows available today for archers to choose from. Anything pulling at least 40 pounds is plenty for deer hunting, but, as mentioned at the beginning of this chapter, lighter draw weights will also do the job. Some states and provinces have minimum draw weights that are permitted for deer hunting. The same is true for centerfire rifles, muzzleloaders, shotguns and handguns. Be sure to check those regulations before deciding what to hunt with.

Since compound bows make it easier for hunters to accurately shoot heavy draw weights, there is a tendency among some serious archers to go as high as 70 pounds or more for hunting. Draw weights in that range generally produce faster arrow speeds and flatter trajectories. A resulting advantage is the ability to use one sight pin for 10 to 20 yard intervals rather than 5 yard increments, which are common for bows with lighter draw weights.

I've found sight pins to be necessary for accurate aiming with bow and arrows, although some people do well by shooting instinctively. If you are just starting out as a hunting archer, you might try both methods to find out which produces the best results for you. A number of pendulum sights designed specifically for tree stand hunting are on the market. Once these sights are properly sighted in, they are supposed to be on target regardless of how far a deer is from a tree.

You will also want to decide if you want to shoot with fingers or a release. Try both and decide which you prefer. Most bowhunters shoot

Recurve and long bows are still popular among traditionalists for stand hunting whitetails. Gene Ballew is shown here wading a river with a recurve on the way to a remote tree stand.

more consistently with a release than fingers, but I prefer to shoot with fingers since that's the way I've always shot a bow and arrow.

Practice as much as possible with archery equipment to maintain proficiency and determine the distances at which you are most accurate. For that matter, practicing as much as possible with guns, especially handguns, is a good idea, too. When hunting, only take shots at ranges that you are confident of making clean kills.

Most hunting arrows are made of aluminum, but carbon shafts are becoming more popular because of their light weight and durability.

Practice makes perfect as far as shooting both bow and arrow and firearms. It's impossible to practice too much when preparing for stand hunting. The more familiar hunters are with their equipment, the better they will be able connect when a shot is offered.

However, carbons are also more expensive. Wooden arrows are preferred by some traditional bowhunters who spend time afield with long or recurve bows.

The most popular broadheads for stand hunting whitetails today are those with presharpened razor blade inserts that weigh between 100 and 125 grains, but I've used heads weighing up to 140 grains. Some of the top brands of broadheads are Bear, Game Tracker, Rocky Mountain, Satellite, Thunderhead, Wasp, Muzzy and Zwickey. Broadheads may fly differently than field points, so be sure to practice with the heads you plan to hunt with before the season begins. Stick with the heads that fly best out of your bow.

Crossbows are not uniformly legal for whitetail hunting like compounds, recurves and long bows are. However, they are legal during regular bow seasons in some provinces and states, with Ohio being a prime example. Many more states allow handicapped hunters to hunt

I used a 150 pound pull Horton crossbow fitted with a one power scope and Game Tracker string to collect this Ohio 6-pointer. Ohio is one state where it's legal to hunt with a crossbow during the regular bow season. I found hunting with a crossbow little different than any other type of bow and arrow.

with crossbows under special permits. I used a 150 pound pull Horton crossbow to arrow a fine 6-pointer in Ohio one fall. That draw weight is standard for deer hunting.

I used a Game Tracker broadhead to shoot the 6-pointer I got with the crossbow, making a liver hit. I also had a Game Tracker string attached to the aluminum arrow I got the buck with, which led me to the carcass about 150 yards from where I made the shot. There was an excellent blood trail to follow even if I hadn't been using a string tracker.

I found that crossbows are not as effective as a lot of novices think they are. The light arrows fall fast, making it essential to know exactly how far away the deer is. A miscalculation of five yards can cause a miss just the same as an arrow launched from any other type of bow. Long shots are less practical with a crossbow than a compound. Arrow speeds from a 150 pound pull crossbow are comparable to a 60 pound pull compound.

When hunting whitetails, I like to use as many different types of guns and bows as possible. Doing so usually allows me to increase my hunting time by participating in a number of different seasons. Regardless of what you're hunting with, however, spending time in a blind or stand is the best way to get a good look and shot at whitetails.

Chapter 11

Scent Control

Your scent is one of the most important considerations in stand hunting. It can make or break a hunt. If the whitetail smells you before you are able to shoot it, your chances of getting that animal are, more often than not, eliminated. When you are set up in such a way that it doesn't wind you, the odds of scoring are in your favor.

In the vast majority of cases where I've been successful stand hunting, including the times I took my biggest bucks, I've been posted downwind from where I expected to see deer and that's where they appeared. Don't forget that. When the wind is in your favor, there is no way a whitetail can detect your presence, as long as you don't

The most important principle of stand hunting is to post downwind from where you expect to see deer. Whitetails that wind hunters may not even show themselves, much less provide the opportunity for a shot.

make noise or movement that gives your position away.

The non-typical 12-pointer I shot in Saskatchewan was 125 yards away and a brisk breeze was blowing from it to me. Had the wind been blowing in the opposite direction, there is a chance that buck might have smelled me, preventing a shot. In fact, a doe and fawn went by first. Had the wind direction been reversed, they might have caught my scent and spooked, preventing me from seeing that buck at all. Whitetails can easily smell a person that far away.

When I shot that Michigan 11-pointer from the ground, he was only about 35 yards away. No other deer led the way for him. However, I know he would have winded me if the air flow were reversed that

Don't forget about thermal air currents when hunting in hilly country. Even when there's no wind, the air tends to rise in the morning as temperatures increase, carrying your scent with it. Thermals normally carry scent downhill during the evening as it cools down.

day, and he probably would have changed directions before I was able to get a shot at him.

It's not always possible to determine from which direction all whitetails will come. I've seen plenty of occasions when bucks showed up where they were least expected. Some deer may wind you under those circumstances. If you are hunting from an elevated stand, the chances of being smelled are reduced, but certainly not eliminated.

By tying a light piece of string or thread on your gun barrel, as shown here, you can keep track of changes in wind direction. The same thing is possible when you are bowhunting, or when a wind indicator can be tied near your stand where it's easy to see. Before deciding where to hunt, you can check wind direction by looking at a flag, smoke, automobile exhaust, vegetation, snow and many other things.

The most important thing to remember is to select a stand site where you are least likely to be winded. If deer smell you with increasing frequency, it's time for a change in locations. Whitetails sometimes learn where a stand is and begin circling downwind of the stand before approaching the area. If that happens, it's a sign a spot has been over-hunted.

Even on days when there is no apparent wind, thermal air currents can carry your scent to whitetails, especially in hilly or mountainous terrain where thermals are most common. Thermals generally carry scent upslope during morning hours. As the air warms up, it rises. As the air cools during the evening, it sinks, carrying scent downslope. Thermals may not affect scent dispersal significantly on days when temperatures are uniform.

When there is a breeze, it's generally not too difficult to determine which direction it is coming from. A flag is flown from one camp I hunt from and part of the prehunt ritual is to look at the flag to see which way it is blowing. Once we know which way the wind is coming from, we can select the stands that will be best for hunting. A weather vane, wind sock or any number of other items can be used to determine wind direction, too.

Smokers often watch which way the smoke drifts from cigarettes to decipher wind flow. Keeping an eye on the exhaust from a warming vehicle, the flame from a lighter, falling snow flakes or the motion of leaves, grass and brush are additional clues. If you have access to a weather station on television or radio, forecasters will often tell you which direction the wind is coming from and if any changes are expected during the course of the day.

While in the field, having a piece of thread or a feather tied to your bow or gun or next to your stand will enable you to keep track of wind direction. If the wind shifts permanently to a direction that proves to be unfavorable for your position, it's always a good idea to change locations to continue to use the wind to your advantage. It can be to your disadvantage not to move if the switch in wind direction increases the chances that approaching whitetails will smell you.

It's also important to reduce your scent as much as possible by staying clean. Showering or bathing with an unscented soap before you go hunting is ideal. Avoid using smelly aftershaves, perfumes or deodorants when deer hunting. These concoctions are made strong enough so they can be smelled by humans. Whitetails don't have any trouble smelling them and they are a dead giveaway that a person is in the area.

When you are hunting out of a camp where there's no running water, taking a sponge bath or using products such as Scent Shield's Body Bath Towels, which are made by Robinson Laboratories from St. Paul, Minnesota, can help you stay as clean as possible. Scent Shield also comes in spray bottles and is one of a number of products on the market that claim to eliminate human odor. I can't tell you if these products are successful in totally eliminating human scent, but I do know that some brands eliminate some odors—and that is a definite benefit for deer hunters. A whitetail's nose is its strongest defense against hunters. Reducing the effectiveness of that defense mechanism, much less eliminating it, can increase a hunter's chances of success.

I have to admit that I've been a skeptic when it comes to scent eliminators, but I tried them nonetheless. The more I use them the more I'm convinced they work. An incident that started to turn my thinking around on these products happened early one morning on the way deer hunting. As I was refueling the vehicle I got gas on my hands. The odor smelled strong to me, and I knew deer wouldn't have any trouble smelling it.

I tried washing the smell off with soap and water, but that didn't work. Fortunately, I had some Scent Shield with me. One application got rid of the gas smell from my hands. I reasoned that if the product got rid of such a stubborn scent, it would work on other odors, too.

Although I didn't shoot a deer that morning, I saw a half dozen animals—including a buck chasing a doe—and none of them detected me. The buck would have been easy to take, but he only had short spikes, so I decided to wait for a bigger one. For best results, Scent Shield and similar products should be sprayed on socks, underwear, boots and hats as well as outer garments. When hunting in cold weather, however, I do not spray the products on socks and under garments to reduce the chances of getting chilled from the moisture.

Another product on the market designed for hunters to eliminate or block their odor is the Scent Lok Suit. There's a layer of charcoal inside the fabric that is supposed to absorb scent from the person wearing the garments. The suit comes with pants, a pullover top and a hood. They are supposed to be worn under normal outer layers of clothing, but when the weather is warm, the suit can serve as an outer layer.

I've had mixed results while wearing the suit. On one occasion when I was wearing the Scent Lok outfit, a doe that was downwind of me seemed to smell me. She stomped a front foot and blew a number of times. However, she may have been reacting to my scent trail from when I approached the tree stand.

On another occasion when I was posted on the ground while bowhunting during September, the suit seemed to work its magic. The spot overlooked several major deer trails, but I was on top of a trail that had less use. I obviously expected deer to walk by on the heavily used trails. In fact, another hunter who had hunted the spot the evening before had seen bucks and does using those trails.

Wearing a Scent Lok suit as this hunter is doing can reduce the chances that whitetails will smell a stand hunter.

As it turned out, a group of deer decided to travel on the minor trail where I sat. An adult doe was in the lead and it was too brushy to try a shot with bow and arrow, so I simply froze. The wind was in my favor as they approached. I thought the doe might spook when she saw me a matter of feet away, but she didn't.

The doe circled around me, ending up downwind and no more than 10 to 15 feet away. I figured she would smell me at that point, but she didn't. A wide 6-pointer was behind the doe. He circled me like the doe had. A smaller buck and a fawn came next.

When the fawn circled behind me, it got even closer than its mother and finally blew my cover. When it did, I'm not sure if it actually smelled me or my scent on the ground from when I had gotten into position. Regardless, that test convinced me that the Scent Lok Suit definitely provides deer hunters an advantage in reducing the chances, if not eliminating them, of whitetails smelling them. For more information about Scent Lok Suits dial 1-800-315-5799, fax 1-616-755-0176 or write to P.O. Box 3972, Muskegon Heights, MI 49444-3972.

While I was hunting with fellow outdoor writer and whitetail fanatic Bill Winke recently, he told me he wears two Scent Lok suits to avoid being smelled by deer.

To reduce the chances of contaminating hunting clothes with foreign odors, you can store outer layers in sealed plastic bags with limbs or branches from local, aromatic evergreen trees. Some hunters only wear garments protected in this fashion while in the field, resealing them in the bag as soon as they reach their vehicle, camp or home. Soiled and sweaty clothing, including hats, should be cleaned to eliminate strong odors.

As mentioned in a previous chapter, Mark Mueller's Invisiblind (3606 Central Ave., Catawissa, MO 63015 [314-257-2804]) is supposed to prevent the escape of human scent, reducing the chances deer will wind hunters who are inside. Rock star Ted Nugent and *Bowhunter Magazine* Editor M. R. James have both had good results while hunting from the blind.

Stand hunters should also consider the odds of whitetails encountering your scent trail after you are in place. I've seen spooky whitetails pick up my scent trail that is as much as two or three hours old. They reacted as though they've bumped into an electric fence. They jump back as if shocked and often go back the way they came.

To reduce the chances of broadcasting your scent where you will be hunting, always try to approach stand sites into or across the wind. At the same time, you want to avoid contaminating the travel routes with your scent where you expect whitetails to wander past your stand. If you have to cross deer trails near your stand, try to jump over them and/or use a cover scent such as fox or coyote urine on your boots.

The urine from these predators smells so strong that it can overshadow any scent you might be leaving while walking to your stand. Whitetails are used to smelling predators common to their area without getting alarmed. Just be sure that the scent you use is from an animal found in the area. Be-

Applying red fox urine to boots or boot pads can help cover the scent a hunter might otherwise leave while walking to a stand.

Stand hunters should approach the spot where they hope to post by traveling into or across the wind, avoiding deer trails that whitetails are expected to use to travel past the stand site.

cause red foxes are widely distributed throughout much of the whitetail's range, urine from them is popular as a cover scent. Where coyotes are abundant, however, there may be few foxes around, so using urine from the more abundant predator may work best.

When hunting during the rut, you may want to use a scent attractive to bucks, such as doe urine, on your boots. Scent can be applied directly to the boots or be worn on a scent pad. An alternative is to drag a pad or rag soaked in scent behind you as you walk to your stand or blind.

The scent of a doe could serve a dual purpose. It could help mask your scent as well as entice a buck to follow you to your post. To be most effective, sex scents should be used only in periods when local does are in heat.

During a hunt I shared one fall in Missouri with Paul Bambenek and his brother Greg, Paul demonstrated the effectiveness of leaving a scent trail with a deer attractant. The pair produces the Dr. Juice line of deer scents. Paul said he squirted Dr. Juice attractant on his boots while walking to his stand, stopping every 75 to 100 yards to reapply the liquid, so the odor would remain as strong at the end of his path as at the start.

After Paul got in position, a 6-point buck appeared, nose to the ground, following right in Paul's footsteps. When the buck was about 100 yards away, it spotted a doe and left the scent trail to join her. Paul decided to take the buck at that point and dropped it with the .50 caliber Knight muzzleloader he was using.

Scents that are attractive to whitetails can be applied to scrapes, as Brent Hunt is doing here, worn on boots or applied to drag rags to help lure bucks within view of your stand.

Brother Greg, who developed the line of deer scents and also goes by the name of Dr. Juice, suggested that hunters who want to leave scent trails leading to their point of ambush might have best results by starting them where they want deer to end up—some place in front of their blind or stand. The reason for this, according to Bambenek, is that whitetails most often follow scent in the direction that it gets stronger. Scent trails are usually strongest at the point of origin and gradually weaken

Greg Bambenek, otherwise known as Dr. Juice, with a Missouri 8-pointer he collected with his third arrow after the whitetail was attracted by scent he put near his stand.

the further they are extended, unless scent is replenished or dripped steadily as the hunter walks.

When leaving scent trails, the manufacturers of both Pete Rickard and Buck Stop scents recommend that before you post you should walk in a circle around your stand site at the distance you would like to get a shot at a deer. They also suggest sprinkling scent on the ground at strategic points where you would like deer to stop. The use of Buck Stop's Doe-in-heat scent played an important role in helping me tag an Ohio 6-pointer one year while hunting with a Horton crossbow.

At first light I put some of the scent in a scrape before getting in position nearby with a portable climbing stand. About an hour later, I saw a buck 100 yards behind me, walking away. Several grunts from a Primos call stopped the whitetail, then he turned and slowly meandered my way.

The buck went out of sight for several minutes. When he reappeared about 40 yards away, he was heading straight for me. The deer

Removing the tarsal glands from whitetails—both bucks and does—you or your friends shoot, can help in the taking of additional deer when the glands are used to leave scent trails or hung near your stand.

fed as it slowly moved forward. When 25 yards away, it turned broadside; I thought about taking a shot, but there were too many leaves and branches in the way that would surely deflect an arrow, so I waited.

Seconds later, the buck suddenly stiffened as though it detected my presence. Thermals may have carried a whiff of my scent to the deer because it moved away from me before turning right on a course that paralleled the lane the scrape was on. If it stayed in the brush, there was no way I could get an arrow to it. But when the whitetail got even with the scrape, it smelled the scent I had left there, and it couldn't resist the odor. The deer walked straight toward the scrape, entering an opening about 20 yards away. That's when I took my shot and scored a solid hit.

On that same Missouri hunt during which Paul Bambenek took a 6-pointer with a muzzleloader after it followed a scent trail he left, brother Greg claimed an 8-pointer with bow and arrow that most certainly would have gotten away if it weren't for the scent he deposited near his stand before he got into position. During that hunt, we took part in the state's last two days of bow season and first two days of gun season. Greg simply squirted some scent on brush 20 yards to the left and right before climbing into his stand. Another way to place scents near stands is to use empty 35 mm film canisters. They can be filled with cotton soaked with scent. The canisters can then be hung near stands to attract whitetails.

The morning of the Missouri hunt, Greg was posted in a tree stand overlooking a large field when the buck walked directly under him. His arrow missed. The deer bounded off a short distance, then stopped, still within easy bow range. Bambenek's second arrow was deflected by a branch and also missed, sending the whitetail 70 yards into the field. The buck was obviously disturbed by Greg's arrows, but it didn't connect the disturbance with the presence of a hunter.

Nervous nonetheless, the whitetail started to wander off, but when it got downwind of some of the scent Greg had squirted on branches, it caught the deer's attention. Dr. Juice said the buck did a lip curl and walked right to the scent to investigate, putting the whitetail in position for a third shot. That arrow was on target, going through both lungs. The buck's behavior was especially satisfying to Greg since he makes the scent that helped him get that deer.

Although commercial scents obviously work, hunters can collect scent from deer they bag to help them connect on additional whitetails. The tarsal glands of both bucks and does are normally covered with the animals' urine during the rut. These glands can be removed by cutting the skin around them. If you are done hunting for the year, the glands can be frozen for use the following year. Hunters who will be spending more time afield can use them while fresh, refrigerating or freezing them in plastic bags between each use.

One fall a cousin of mine shot a mature buck in one area and removed one of its tarsal glands to take with him when he hunted another area a day or two later. He dragged the gland behind him on a string while walking to his blind. Later that morning, a 10-pointer appeared following the scent of the foreign buck. My cousin filled his second tag with that whitetail. The 10-pointer was obviously curious about the scent of an unfamiliar, competing buck and went to investigate.

The tarsal gland from a doe will also attract bucks during the rut. One fall while hunting in Saskatchewan with guide Mike Aftanas, I took the tarsal gland from a doe he shot and hung it from a tree in front of my stand. Hours later, a mature 8-pointer appeared from downwind to check out the "doe" he thought he was smelling. It cost him his life.

Hunters can collect urine from bucks and does during field dressing and can bottle it for later use. Be sure to bring an empty bottle with you if you plan on collecting urine from dead whitetails. Urine from bucks works well for making mock scrapes. Doe urine can also be added to scrapes to attract bucks.

Lee Rotzien is the president of a Michigan-based company that sells deer urine under the trade name of "Lee's." He said the only additive he uses in the urine is an odorless chemical that prevents fermentation. Deer urine will break down quickly, especially if exposed to heat and sunlight. Hunters who have urine or urine-based products left at the end of the season should freeze them, so they will still be potent for the next year's hunt.

Rotzien told me that he bagged a Pope and Young buck on opening day (October 1) of Michigan's bow season as a result of making a mock scrape with buck urine prior to the opener. He said he had made a mock scrape using the scent the week before, and the book buck had its nose in the scrape when he arrowed it on the first day of the season. Lee explained that he had used a rake to make the scrape under an appropriate limb. Scent had been deposited in the scrape and on the overhanging branch. A Q-tip cotton swab had then been dipped in the concentrated urine and tied to the limb above the scrape.

Lee said he was hunting during the evening from a tree stand overlooking the scrape when a bush 40 yards to his right started shaking violently. Moments later, the 10-pointer came walking toward him with leaves on its antlers. The big buck approached slowly, stopping to smell the air four or five times before reaching the scrape.

"He was stretched out like a dog on point when I shot him," Lee commented.

The buck's antlers had a final score of 131 with only two inches of deductions.

The use of scents may not always make or break a hunt, but they can make a difference some of the time, so smart hunters will add them to their arsenal of accessories. However, how you control your scent will almost always be a deciding factor in the outcome of a hunt for whitetails from a blind or stand. Try not to forget that. If you do, the deer will more than likely remind you!

Chapter 12

Sights and Sounds

About 6:00 p.m. one evening last fall while I was bowhunting from a tree stand in Wisconsin, I heard a gray squirrel barking behind me. All squirrels have a habit of barking or chattering when startled. I turned toward the disturbed squirrel in an effort to determine what was responsible for its outburst.

After scanning its surroundings carefully, I finally spotted a whitetail doe silhouetted against a white birch tree. Standing motionless, the deer was partially obscured by limbs and leaves. The doe probably had surprised the squirrel on the ground. That's why the bushytail was barking at it.

The whitetail was about 75 yards away. It eventually walked out of sight. I probably never would have known the animal was there if it hadn't been for that squirrel. As it turned out, there

A barking gray squirrel tipped me off to the presence of a whitetail behind me on a Wisconsin hunt. Other animals and birds can warn stand hunters about the appearance of deer, too.

was no chance for a shot at that deer. I would have had the advantage, if it had come my way. Simply seeing that whitetail, however, helped make the evening more enjoyable.

One of the main objectives of stand hunting is to see and/or hear deer before they detect your presence. This takes concentration. In many cases, a flash of movement, an out-of-place patch of color or the sound of another bird or mammal (like that Wisconsin gray squirrel), may be your first clue that a deer is nearby.

Red squirrels are notorious for scolding critters that invade their space. Red squirrels have tipped me off to the presence of more deer than have gray squirrels. Neither species of squirrel *always* barks or chatters at whitetails, but they do often enough to be worth checking out. They could just as easily be complaining about the presence of another hunter or a wild predator such as a coyote, bobcat or fox.

The sound of squirrels walking or digging through dry leaves on the ground can resemble the noise deer make while walking or feeding—

Whitetails like this yearling buck are often easy to hear when walking in dry leaves. Always assume such sounds are made by a deer, until you confirm otherwise.

and vice versa. It's common to have plenty of squirrels in oak woods where acorns are abundant. Whenever you hear the sound of an animal in the leaves, assume it's a deer until you find out otherwise. Always look toward the source of the sound, and be ready to prepare for a shot.

On at least two occasions, I assumed noises I heard in the leaves were made by squirrels because I had seen squirrels there earlier. But spike bucks were responsible for the disturbance in both cases. Hunting from the ground with a rifle in Michigan one of those times, I was caught by surprise when the buck instead of a squirrel walked into view. The whitetail saw and/or smelled me. His reflexes were faster than mine, and he got away. Had I been prepared for the appearance of a deer—as I should have been—I could have shot that whitetail.

The second time this happened, I was bowhunting from a ladder stand in Georgia. When the buck appeared I was just as surprised as I had been in Michigan, but this time the whitetail didn't detect me. I managed to tag this buck.

The sound of steady footsteps in the leaves often signals an approaching whitetail. Cautious deer will routinely pause, sometimes for long periods, after walking a short distance. If leaves are wet, the sound of a snapping twig may be the only warning that a deer is coming.

The sound of rustling leaves and a snapped twig are what alerted me to the presence of the trophy 11-pointer I shot from the ground in Michigan. As soon as I heard the noise I got ready to raise my rifle. My rifle was leaning against the tree next to me. I had time to grab it before the deer came into view. As soon as I saw the deer was a good buck, I took the safety off as I shouldered my Remington .30-06.

Whitetails walking on crunchy, crusted snow make almost as much noise as whitetails walking on dry leaves. The deer seem to know it, too, because they usually move cautiously, stopping every few feet to listen and smell for danger. I'm sure the noise they make while walking impairs their hearing. Snow often becomes crusted and icy on well-packed runways before it does elsewhere, making it easier for hunters to hear animals using these trails.

Where standing water is common—such as swamps—the sound of sloshing or splashing water can give away the presence of whitetails. When temperatures drop below freezing, the ice that forms on the surface of water makes even more noise when it breaks under the weight of traveling deer. Hunters in stands near muddy areas should listen for the sucking sound of hooves being pulled from the muck.

Deer running through woods make crashing sounds accompanied by the noise of snapping twigs. The vibration caused by hooves pounding the ground can be heard at times, too, especially in open habitat where this noise isn't overpowered by louder sounds. Running deer can appear quickly and be gone just as fast, so it's important to be ready if you want to have a chance for a shot. Whitetails that have been running may stop suddenly, too, so be prepared for that possibility. A loud whistle may bring running deer to a halt for a standing shot.

Deer make vocalizations that stand hunters can sometimes hear before they see them. Buck grunts and fawn bleats are the vocalizations I've heard most often. While trailing or tending does during the rut, bucks make a grunting sound. A number of calls on the market imitate this sound. It is also recorded on numerous deer hunting videos. If you hear a buck grunting nearby, get ready.

Grunt calls are commonly used by hunters today, so the grunt you hear may be from another hunter instead of a deer. Always be sure of your target before attempting a shot. The origin of all sounds should be verified by sight to confirm they were indeed made by a whitetail.

When fawns become separated from their mothers, they may call loudly in an effort to relocate them. The high-pitched bleats, also imitated by some commercial calls, are distinctive, but these calls can vary

I shot this heavy-beamed 12-pointer in Manitoba soon after hearing a fawn call for its mother. This buck or another one had probably chased the fawn away from its mother, intent on breeding her.

from one fawn to another. Fawns often are chased away by bucks during the rut, so if you hear or see a fawn looking for its mother, it's an indication some breeding may be going on nearby. You should standby for some action.

One November while hunting from a tree stand in Manitoba, I heard a fawn bleating. Minutes later, a huge buck walked by and I shot him. The 12-pointer weighed 285 pounds.

Hunters will probably hear more often than grunts and bleats, the snorts and blowing sounds whitetails make when alarmed or alerted. They make the sound by blowing air through their nostrils. It serves as a warning to other deer in the area. Deer blow most often when they smell and/or see a hunter. Whitetails frequently run after snorting. They may continue making the sound while moving. Animals that don't feel as though they are in immediate danger will sometimes snort and stomp a front hoof numerous times while remaining in one spot.

It is occasionally possible to spot a blowing deer and get a shot at it. Your best chance at a snorting deer will be when it moves your way after pinpointing another hunter. The warning sound will help prepare you to see the whitetail.

Blue jays and other species of birds call attention to intruders by

squawking or screaming at them. They pay more attention to hawks, owls, ground-based predators and people than deer, but they do occasionally scold whitetails. More often, birds such as grouse and ducks that have been flushed by approaching deer have helped tip me off to their presence.

Howling wolves played a role on a deer hunt in Manitoba one year when I shot a respectable 11-pointer. Besides giving me a thrill, the sound of the wolves pushed deer toward me. It was November 8, opening day

On another Manitoba hunt, I think howling wolves contributed to my success. Three bucks came by me from the direction the wolves were within a span of 30 minutes. I shot the third one, which had 11 points and weighed 250 pounds.

of the province's firearm season; I was on my second hunt with Buddy Chudy's Mantagao Outfitters. I was 10 to 12 feet from the ground in one of his stands when the wolves howled to the west soon after daylight.

Within a matter of minutes after the howling faded, I saw the legs of a deer coming from the west. The stand was in a clump of spruce trees. Some of the evergreens blocked the whitetail's body from view. It was easy to see movement of brown legs against the white of a few inches of snow on the ground.

When the deer walked into an opening, I saw that it was a buck. With a small 8-point rack, the deer was smaller than I wanted to shoot. I had made up my mind before the season opened to shoot only bucks that had at least 10 points.

About 30 minutes after the small 8-pointer went by, another buck with a larger 8-point rack came from the same direction. When in front of me, that whitetail stopped and looked back to the west. Seconds later, I heard, then saw, a third deer coming from the direction the wolves had been howling. Amazingly, that deer was also a buck with an even bigger rack. I counted the tines through my scope and saw five per side.

When the buck stepped into an opening 40 yards away, a shot from my .50 caliber Knight muzzleloader dropped him instantly. One of the buck's brow tines was forked, giving it a total of 11 points. That deer weighed 250 pounds in the round.

Nearby drives being conducted by other hunters or dogs can bring deer your way. It's usually obvious when a noisy drive is underway. Driving hunters normally call out to their partners and try to mimic the sound of barking dogs, so their progress can be monitored.

The sound of dogs chasing deer is also easy to determine. Although this practice is only legal in parts of the south, stray dogs or those that run free sometimes chase deer. Be sure to check local regulations about the legality of shooting deer ahead of free roaming dogs.

Follow the gaze of whitetails and other animals in front of you to help you spot others. Since their senses are keener than ours, they will often detect an approaching whitetail before we can. Does that are being followed by a buck will frequently look behind them.

Watching the actions of deer and other animals in front of you can help tip you off to the approach of whitetails. Deer frequently look toward other approaching deer, as did that second 8-pointer in Manitoba. More often, you will see a doe that's being followed by a buck turn and look back to check on his progress. The buck may not always be in the doe's sight when she does this.

The habit of looking at other deer will frequently be exhibited by feeding whitetails, too. When the animal or animals that are eating are about to be joined by one or more deer, they usually look at them to find out if they recognize them in much the same way that people in a restaurant glance at customers who walk in the door or are about to be seated. Since other deer are normally closer to the action, have better hearing than we do and often have a better view, it's always a good idea to follow their gaze.

A running doe and fawn clued me in to the 12-point non-typical I shot in Saskatchewan during 1993. Those deer were too far away to hear, but their movement across the landscape caught my eye right away. When the rut is on, the sighting of a running doe is always a good reason to get ready for action.

A friend of mine who has poor hearing said he routinely takes cues from animals to help him see deer. On a hunt we shared, he credited the actions of a raccoon eating corn in front of him with tipping him off to the presence of an approaching deer.

The sound of a nearby shot may be a warning that one or more whitetails are coming your way. Always get ready, just in case. Doing so paid off handsomely for Mike Burger from Ann Arbor, Michigan, during November of 1993. He collected a buck with the highest scoring typical rack taken in the state that year, a 10-pointer scoring 174 7/8.

On the evening of the fourth day of gun season Mike heard a shot that wasn't far away. Instinctively, he looked in that direction when he heard the gun go off. About a minute later, he saw a whitetail approaching through the woods from where the shot had been. The sunlight reflecting from the antlers on the deer's head revealed that it was a buck.

Mike said the whitetail wasn't running, but it was moving at a brisk pace. He thought the deer was headed for a ravine in front of him at first, but it stayed on the far side and headed north. The buck was about 100 yards from Burger.

"At the time I knew it was the biggest buck I ever shot at," Mike said, "but I had no idea how big he really was."

The hunter had the scope mounted on his 12 gauge shotgun set on two power to increase his field of view.

"I picked openings in the brush where the buck was headed and put the cross hairs on them. When he reached the opening, I was ready to shoot. When the cross hairs were on his shoulder, I touched it off.

"I shot twice. I didn't notice any reaction on the first shot. After the second shot, I didn't see or hear anything."

Mike scanned the area where the buck had been with his binoculars but did not see him. Mike then climbed down into the ravine and started toward where the whitetail had been. When in the bottom of the ravine, he spotted a brown mass 40 yards away. A check with the binoculars verified it was the dead buck.

"The buck fell against a tree on the very edge of the ravine," Mike said. "The sides of the ravine were steep at that point. I'm glad he didn't fall in. It would have been tough to get him out.

Jeff Hayford with the mount of a trophy 11-pointer he shot when he was 14. The sound from a nearby road of a vehicle suddenly braking to avoid hitting the buck helped Jeff spot it as it was coming his way.

"We later found out both of my shots hit the buck. The first one hit the heart and the second one broke his back. When I reached the fallen buck and saw how big he was, I think I said, 'Oh my God!'"

If you are hunting near a road, the sound of a vehicle braking suddenly or a honking horn may be a clue that a whitetail is approaching. I sometimes honk at deer I see along highways while driving in an effort to scare them back in the woods as much as to alert them to my presence. Jeff Hayford was posted 70 yards from a paved road in Michigan's Branch County on opening day of firearm season one year when the sound of squealing tires on the road caught his attention.

When he looked toward the sound he saw a huge buck coming toward him. The whitetail had just crossed the road and the driver of a pickup truck pulling a horse trailer slammed on the brakes to avoid hitting it. The deer was only nine yards away when Jeff pointed his 20 gauge pump shotgun at its shoulder and fired. Shot through the heart, the animal started to buckle, but the young hunter (Jeff was 14 years old at the time) was wisely taking no chances and shot a second time, putting another slug through its neck. The 11-pointer's rack scored 170 1/8.

The sound of bucks fighting may also be heard by stand hunters. It's an obvious indication that at least two bucks are nearby. These bouts don't normally last long, so it's usually a good idea to remain where you are and hope at least one of the bucks comes by you when the fight breaks up. Due to the popularity of rattling today, you could be fooled by another hunter staging a fake fight. If the sounds of clashing antlers persists, however, and you're convinced it's the real thing, you might want to investigate. A pair of bucks may have their antlers locked.

I've talked to hunters who have successfully moved in on fighting bucks and taken at least one of the animals. Others, including myself, have been unsuccessful. While stand hunting I've heard a pair of serious buck fights, one in Saskatchewan and the other in North Dakota. The Saskatchewan battle lasted so long that I eventually climbed out of the tree

Get ready for action if you hear bucks fighting nearby. It could mean at least two bucks are close, but it could be another hunter rattling, too. Most fights or sparring matches don't last long. If you hear a pair of bucks going at it for a long time, their antlers might be locked.

stand and went to investigate, convinced the bucks' antlers were locked together. I spotted a doe close to where the action was and backed off rather than risk spooking her. The fight broke up soon afterward.

Based on my experience in Canada, I remained in my North Dakota tree stand when a serious buck fight broke out behind me one morning. I was bowhunting at the time and felt the limited range of my equipment would put me at a disadvantage. I did see one or two bucks that day, but they didn't come within bow range. I'm not sure if either one of them were involved in the fight.

I did get a shot at a nice buck from the same stand the next morning. My arrow missed the whitetail, however, shaving some white hairs off of its belly.

The sound of bucks rubbing their antlers on saplings or trees can sometimes be heard by stand hunters. The noise made when bone contacts wood is distinct. Limbs may be broken during the process. Hunters might see and hear the tree or trees shaking, which can help in pinpointing a buck's location. This sound can't be heard from far away. Neither can the noise of a buck making a scrape. Scrape making in leaves can resemble the sound of a deer walking or a squirrel digging for acorns.

Stand hunters should be alert for any sound that may telegraph the presence of a deer. If you are unsure what is responsible for a sound, try your best to find out by looking toward its origin and continuing to listen. The more sounds you are able to recognize, the better you will become as a deer hunter.

The same is true for movements. Train your eyes to identify the source of every movement. With practice, it will become easier to determine when a whitetail is responsible for the motion.

Spotting a deer is often like putting a puzzle together visually. In many cases, only a portion of a whitetail's anatomy will be visible. You may only see the flicker of an ear, the swish of a tail or the glint of an antler. By concentrating on that piece of the puzzle to figure out where it belongs, the rest of the animal can often be put together piece by piece.

Look for out-of-place horizontal lines that could be the back or belly of a deer. The white coloration of a whitetail's belly, rump or up-lifted tail stands out in most habitat. Deer often flag with their tails when running, but they also lift their tails when defecating. Does may elevate their tails to make it easier for fawns or bucks to follow them in low light situations. Most whitetails also have white throat patches that may be visible.

Never shoot at a patch of white unless you are absolutely sure it is part of a deer! Hunters sometimes use white handkerchiefs or tissue. White undergarments may be visible while their wearers are answering a call of nature or shedding layers as temperatures rise. Even if you determine that a patch of white belongs to a deer, the one on the throat is the only recommended target. The throat patch should only be used by accurate shooters confident of hitting such a small spot. Hunters should never shoot at the tail of a fleeing deer.

Most whitetails are brown or gray in color during hunting seasons. If you see a patch of that color that may belong to a deer, examine it closely to see if it moves or if you can make out another piece of the puzzle. Binoculars make it a lot easier to sort out suspicious-looking colors and lines, even in thick cover. The telescopic sight on a rifle or shotgun should only be used to get a better look at an object when you are sure you are looking at a deer or other animal.

In states and provinces with early deer seasons that open when whitetails still have their reddish summer coats, the animals are easier to see because they contrast sharply with the green vegetation. South Carolina's gun season, for example, begins on August 15—at least in parts of the state. I hunted with Hayward Simmons out of his Cedar Knoll Hunt Club one year. I didn't have any trouble seeing deer from his stands. The antlers of most bucks were still in velvet at that time.

The longer hunters occupy a stand or blind, the more familiar they will become with their surroundings. This increases their chances of spotting anything new, such as a whitetail that walked into their sphere of influence while they were looking the other way. By concentrating on every part of the environment around them (perhaps estimating the distance to items that stand out), hunters will automatically commit to memory the inanimate objects nearby. When a new object such as a deer appears, it usually will be recognized immediately.

Chapter 13

How to Wait for Whitetails

Here is the best way to wait for whitetails: Be full of anticipation that a deer you want will appear during your vigil, but recognize that you don't know exactly when or where it will show up. Such an expectation is sure to keep you alert and help you concentrate on your surroundings so you won't miss the treasured moment when the deer finally does appear. I came to this realization while stand hunting near home.

Stand hunters should always be confident of seeing a whitetail they want while posted. The unknown is where and when that deer will appear. That's what you are there to find out. If you know that someone is tracking a big buck in the area that you might see, as I did during a recent hunt, it helps keep you alert and ready for action.

The date was November 18, the fourth day of Michigan's gun deer season. There was fresh snow on the ground. Before first light I reached my chosen post on a ridge bordering a swamp. About an hour after daylight, two other hunters who had permission to hunt the property appeared, and one of them walked up to me.

"I don't mean to interfere with your hunting," he said, "but I wanted to tell you that a big buck followed your tracks after you walked in this morning. The deer turned to the south. My brother is going to track him to see if he can bring him back around. You're in a good spot here. The two of us are going to post up the trail a ways. Good luck," he concluded. He rejoined his partner and they disappeared up the trail.

Far from interfering with my hunting, the other hunter inspired me. He emphasized the words "BIG BUCK" as he spoke. The words conjured up visions of a heavy bodied whitetail with an equally impressive set of antlers. The deer's tracks had to be huge for the guy to know it was a big buck. If I was lucky, I might actually see the animal as a result of his brother's efforts.

For at least the next two hours, my normal level of anticipation was heightened. I most often hunt where I know there's a minimum of one big boy around. But I seldom have any clue that a trophy animal is on the move nearby until I actually see it. Having advance notice that one might be coming my way was a luxury that kept me on my toes.

I constantly scanned my surroundings for any sign of a moving whitetail, swiveling my head slowly from left to right and back again from right to left, like an owl looking for prey. The routine was only in-

It's fine to crank a scope up to full power while sighting a rifle, shotgun or handgun, but when you are posted, low power is better so you will have the largest field of view possible when a whitetail suddenly appears. Once a deer is sighted and it will be around for a while, there will be plenty of time to turn up the scope's magnification, if necessary.

terrupted when an unidentifiable sight or sound was detected. My eyes were immediately diverted in the direction of any suspicious sound. Any movement I spotted in the surrounding woods got equal attention. The routine reconnaissance resumed after identifying as nonwhitetail related the source of the sight or sound.

My Remington Model 700 .30-06 was in my hands, ready for use at a moment's notice. If the trailed whitetail came by me, he would probably be moving at a steady pace. There wouldn't be much time for a shot, if the opportunity presented itself, and I wanted to be ready. After many years of stand hunting for whitetails, I know only too well how fleeting a chance can be. Many hunters have missed seeing bucks by looking in the wrong direction as the animal passed by. I'm sure it's happened to me, too, but by being vigilant I try to minimize the odds.

I prefer variable scopes in 3-9 power on my rifles. They are set on the lowest magnification most of the time to give me the widest field of view so I can find a whitetail quickly. This is especially important if the deer is walking or running. A moving target can be really hard to find in a scope set on high power, with its limited field of view. There's plenty of time to crank up the magnification on a variable scope to get a better look, if a deer is spotted that's stopped or moving slowly.

Stand hunters who are alert and comfortable, as well as those who expect the arrival of a whitetail at any time, have the best chance of scoring.

Always remember to return a variable scope to a low power after you check out a whitetail. Failure to do so cost a relative of mine a shot at a buck. He had his scope set on maximum magnification when a buck came trotting by at close range. He never did find the whitetail in his sights before it was gone.

It's impossible to wait for whitetails for any length of time and only move your head. The need to change positions and shift your feet is inevitable. And it's not practical to hold a gun or bow in

Hang a bow or gun on a limb or screw-in hook, where it's handy, while waiting for action, to reduce movement and prevent your hands and arms from getting tired. An arrow should be on the string ready to go, as shown here. You will want to have the gun or bow in hand as soon as you see or hear a deer as well as during times of peak activity.

One of the first things you should do after you are situated in your stand or blind when gun hunting is to put a shell in the chamber. If you are using a semi-auto action, make sure it's closed all the way and ready to fire.

the same position all the time, either. Simply try to make sure the coast is clear before you make a move. Timing of moves may not be critical when you are in a tree stand or ground blind because your chances of being seen are reduced—but timing is important when you are more exposed.

If the spot where you are posting has been properly prepared and you're wearing suitable clothing, slight shifts in position should make little, if any, noise. When you do move, try to do it slowly. I've learned that it's important not to hold guns or bows long enough that you're shifting them from one hand to the other every few minutes or that your hands and arms become fatigued. Hang or rest your weapons nearby where they can be grabbed in an instant. I always carry screw-in hooks from which to hang guns or bows. If you are alert, there usually will be time to pick a gun or bow up for a shot once a deer is sighted.

When hunting with bow and arrow, after I get in position, I always have an arrow on the string, ready to go—whether the bow's in my hands or hanging. When hunting with a gun, one of the first things I do after I'm situated in a stand or blind is to load the firearm. I've spoken to a number of hunters who had deer get away because they forgot to do that until too late. They didn't realize their mistake until they tried to shoot and nothing happened.

If you are hunting with a semi-automatic rifle or shotgun, make sure the action is all the way forward and fully cocked when you put a round in the chamber. Hunters who failed to do that have been in for a surprise when they tried to shoot. A few of them who recognized the problem were able to cock the gun in time for a shot, but most weren't.

When hunting with a muzzleloader, I cock the gun and put a cap on the nipple, then put the safety on while I wait for action. If I'm hunting with a black powder rifle on which the hammer serves as the safety, I lower the hammer on a capped nipple and then cock the hammer when I anticipate getting a shot. If the hammer makes a lot of noise when it's cocked, I may leave the gun cocked and wait to put a cap on the nipple when I'm about to shoot—this makes less noise and would be less likely to spook a nearby whitetail.

When you hang a gun or bow, it's easier to keep your hands warm in cold weather. I often keep my gloved hands in my pants pockets when temperatures are cold.

If you have to cough or sneeze and you can't suppress it, hold your hands over your face to muffle the sound as much as possible and/or turn away from where you suspect deer might be. When I'm in a blind and I have to

Eating can help pass some time while you are posted as well as controlling hunger—but make sure the coast is clear before you start eating and move slowly. Food should be wrapped in quiet materials and cut into small, snack size portions to prevent being distracted too long from watching and listening for whitetails.

sneeze or cough, I bend down below the level of windows, too, so the sides help muffle the sound further.

If you have a persistent cough, carry cough drops with you. Sucking on hard candy can help you eliminate a tickly throat and reduce the chances of coughing. You can reduce the noise and movement involved with using cough drops or candy by putting a supply of unwrapped pieces in a clear plastic sandwich bag.

Eating on stand can help pass the time and keep you alert. By satisfying your hunger, eating also keeps you in position for success as long as possible. Sandwiches and other foods should be wrapped in quiet, easily opened materials. Sandwich bags are great for this purpose, too, and cellophane wrap or aluminum foil aren't bad either. Cutting food into small portions makes it easier to eat without being distracted for very long.

To avoid leaving any more scent than necessary at a stand site, I used to carry an empty plastic bottle to urinate in. I've since learned that precaution isn't always necessary. I've spoken to a number of hunters who have seen whitetails stop to investigate human urine deposited near stands. Hunters who are concerned about contaminating the hunting area with urine should carry bottles, cans or Zip Lok bags with them so the liquid can be carried a safe distance from the area to be emptied.

I know some stand hunters who have also defecated in Zip Lok bags when the need arose. A more popular procedure is to dig a hole to deposit the waste in an out-of-the-way location. I prefer to walk as far as possible away from a stand site for a bowel movement. And don't forget to take your gun or bow with you when nature calls.

A range finder, like the one this bowhunter is using, is ideal for determining yardages to specific landmarks once you are in position. You can improve your distance-estimating ability by comparing your estimates with range finder readings.

Some hunters help pass time while waiting for whitetails in a blind by reading, as does this bowhunter. Readers should try not to get too involved in the text. If they do, they risk not seeing deer that would have otherwise been seen.

On two occasions while performing bodily functions I've seen bucks. One was a forkhorn that I wasn't interested in shooting. The second, however, was a trophy buck that I wanted to shoot. Since I had a muzzleloader with me, I could have taken a shot, but the whitetail never presented me with an ideal shot for the front loader. Had I been at my post, I'm confident I would have gotten that deer.

Several gun hunters I know help pass the time on stand by counting the shots they hear during the course of the day. This preoccupation gives them something to occupy their minds while waiting for whitetails to appear. They do it primarily during the first days of the season when most shots are fired. They pay particular attention to shots they hear nearby, which could mean a whitetail is headed their way.

Bowhunters who haven't familiarized themselves with the distance to landmarks before getting in a stand can use a range finder to gather that information while waiting. Range finders are perfect for determining how far away objects are without having to pace the distance off and leave your scent on the ground. They offer the only accurate means of figuring out how far away a deer is while it's still in sight. A good way to improve your ability to accurately estimate distances is to make a guess when you spot an object or animal and then compare the estimate with the range finder reading.

Other hunters keep themselves occupied while in blinds by reading or listening to a radio with ear plugs. Some stand hunting readers look up after finishing a paragraph while others complete a page between glances. I have occasionally resorted to reading while in a blind during lulls in deer activity. I have a hard time concentrating on what I'm reading because I'm afraid I'm going to miss something. I would never consider listening to a radio because I rely on my hearing too much.

In addition to occupying your time on stand, using deer calls and rattling antlers or bags can improve your chances of seeing or shooting a whitetail. Both calling and rattling are most effective on days with light to moderate breezes, so the sound carries well. For obvious reasons, rattling is not recommended during gun hunts on public land when other hunters are nearby.

Calls that imitate a buck grunt or doe bleat are most effective for attracting a buck's attention. Does most often respond to calls that imitate fawns. Some adjustable calls can be used to make all three sounds. Carrying more than one call can be an advantage if you want to produce the sounds of a buck and doe or a pair of bucks without having to fool around with adjustments. The calls from a couple of different deer will sometimes arouse the curiosity of a whitetail more effectively than the sounds produced by one call.

By blowing calls every 15 to 30 minutes, you may lure a deer into view that you might not otherwise have seen. I called in a beautiful 8-pointer with a doe bleat while hunting in Alabama during January. Calls can also come in handy for bringing deer back that got by the first time or are out of range. While bowhunting in Georgia, I used a buck grunt to lure into bow range an aggressive forkhorn that had been trying to start a fight with a pair of spikehorns. Unfortunately, my arrow missed when I took the shot.

When it comes to rattling, I prefer to carry a rattling bag rather than antlers because the bag is easier to transport in a backpack. The product I use is made by Woods Wise. After more than four hours had gone by without a deer sighting one November while bowhunting in Manitoba with Buddy Chudy's Mantagao Outfitters, I decided to see if I could stir things up by rattling during the afternoon. Barely five minutes after I finished the sequence, a tre-

Using a grunt tube or call is a good way to spend time in a stand, as long as it's not windy. A call can help bring whitetails into view that might not otherwise have been seen, bring those back that disappeared before a shot was possible or lure deer closer that are out of range.

Nick Sisley with a pair of 9-pointers he grunted in with a Knight & Hale grunt tube in Georgia.

mendous buck that would have scored at least in the 150s trotted into
view, headed right for me.

Unfortunately, the whitetail turned to follow the tracks of a doe that
had been by my stand earlier, never presenting me with the chance for
a bow shot. If I would have had a rifle instead, the outcome would have
been different. I have rattled in at least one buck that I shot with a rifle
while stand hunting.

The best way to spend time while stand hunting for whitetails, of
course, is to have deer and other wildlife in sight most of the time.
There's seldom the opportunity to get bored when game is abundant
during most of your vigil. Time goes by quickly under those circumstances and the odds of seeing a deer you want are increased, too. If

Rattling is another tactic to lure whitetails into view while stand hunting, provided other hunters aren't nearby or you are hunting private land where you won't be disturbed. I prefer a Woods Wise Rattler Bag for rattling to antlers.

the rut is underway, pay particular attention to does and their backtrail that you see while posted. A trailing buck could show up at any time. Does that appear to be running from something or that look behind them are most likely being courted.

Non-target wildlife such as grouse, turkeys, other birds, small mammals such as squirrels and weasels and predators have often kept me entertained and on my toes while stand hunting. Wildlife of all types provide a pleasant diversion in the absence of whitetails. You can learn as much about other creatures as deer while you're posted.

The basic premise that stand hunting is based on is: you will eventually see one or more deer while posted, provided the location has

There's plenty of opportunity to observe other wildlife while waiting for whitetails and these critters can often keep hunters entertained. I've frequently watched ruffed grouse like this one eat tree buds for long periods of time, but I've been fortunate enough to see a long list of other animals, too, just like most other stand hunters.

been properly chosen and you have enough patience. The wait for the right whitetail can be measured in days or weeks rather than hours. That non-typical 12-pointer I shot with a muzzleloader in Saskatchewan, for example, was taken on my fourth full day of hunting. However, I had been waiting for more than 25 years of stand hunting for a whitetail of that caliber. On other hunts, I've spent more than a week in the field before taking a buck or doe. Patience is one of the most important qualities that stand hunters should cultivate.

It's ideal if you can post from first to last light day after day. Such persistence normally produces results. However, it isn't necessary to be that patient to consistently score from a blind or tree stand. If you can only handle posting for periods of two to four hours at a time, that's good enough. Most hunters seldom spend more than that in a stand at one time.

Stand hunters should always be confident about seeing whitetails while posted. However, as mentioned at the beginning of this chapter, you seldom know when or where the right one will appear. That's what we are there to find out. It's nice to get an advance warning, as I did, about a hunter tracking a big buck in the vicinity, but that doesn't happen often. It should be taken for granted that whitetails will be moved by other hunters, whether or not there's snow on the ground. It should also be taken for granted deer will be moving on their own for feeding or breeding purposes while we are posted. In all cases there's an excellent chance we will see them during the course of their travels.

As mentioned in the first chapter of this book, one of the major advantages of stand hunting is it's easy for anyone to learn. However, there's a lot more involved in waiting for whitetails than a lot of hunters realize. That's why some hunters are better at it than others. Many of the finer points of stand hunting are learned with experience over time.

This chapter can help speed up that process by explaining many of the things I've learned during 30 years of stand hunting that have contributed to my success. Information in this chapter also includes tips from hundreds of successful stand hunters that I've interviewed over those years. One of the most important things that stand hunters can bring with them to whitetail country is the right mental attitude.

A positive mental attitude is one of the most important attributes a stand hunter can have. Optimism, confidence, concentration, patience and persistence are all parts of that attitude.

Your mind should be as prepared as the blind, stand or spot where you will be waiting. Much of the preparation before the hunt begins should contribute to a *positive mental attitude.*

You should have *confidence* in the spot you will be hunting, based on scouting or the efforts of a friend, family member or guide. Confidence breeds *optimism.* You should be optimistic about seeing deer, recognizing a realistic probability that you might be able to shoot one of them sometime during your hunt. An optimist who doesn't fill a tag one day remains confident he or she will eventually do so, taking one day at a time. Optimists begin each day confident their hunt will be satisfying even if they don't see or shoot a whitetail, knowing that each day afield puts them closer to their goal.

Personally, I enjoy every day that I have the opportunity to hunt whitetails. I always feel better, more alive, when I'm playing the role of predator in deer couantry. And there's seldom, if ever, a day when I'm afield that I don't learn or experience something new and different. I like that. It's rare for me to end a day of deer hunting without being grateful for having had the chance to spend time afield, regardless of the outcome.

Confidence and optimism contribute to two more important mental attributes that can be essential for consistent stand hunting success—*patience* and *persistence.* Stand hunters who know they have an excellent chance of seeing deer often have the patience it takes to stay put until it happens. Those who are confident/optimistic will be persistent, hunting day after day until they are successful.

Although not as important as the other qualities mentioned so far, *concentration* on your surroundings can be helpful. At each new stand site, I try to become completely familiar with the sights and sounds around me. That's the best way to be able to notice any changes created by the arrival of one or more whitetails. One of the main objectives of stand hunting is to see and/or hear deer before they detect your presence. It often takes concentration to do that. Hints on what to listen and look for are included in the previous chapter.

Part of a *positive mental attitude* toward stand hunting for whitetails is the realization that it isn't necessary to shoot a deer in order to have a satisfying hunt. The fact is, you will spend more days afield when you *don't* shoot a deer than days when you do. This is true for everyone, myself included, and it is important to accept this as part of deer hunting. If your hunt or season ends with an unfilled tag, it doesn't mean you are a failure. Contrary to the impression you might get from reading outdoor magazines, the majority of deer hunters do not score on every hunt, so you're not alone.

While reading this book, you might even get the impression that I always succeed because I concentrate on mentioning the deer I've shot. The objective of this book is to tell you about tactics that work, not those that haven't. I assure you that I've either failed to shoot a deer or chosen not to on plenty of hunts.

Take it from me that it is possible to have a great hunt even though no arrows are released or no shots fired. The quality of a hunt should be judged by many other factors that are part of the total experience: enjoying the company of friends and relatives, hunting a new area, learning or experiencing something new. I view every hunt as a learning experience, and I'm seldom disappointed. Hunters who insist on killing a deer in order to be successful often miss out on the finer pleasures of deer hunting. It's okay to do everything possible to try to shoot a deer, as long as it's legal, but when you don't succeed it's important to accept it and look forward to the next time, when you may want to do things differently.

Hunters with a positive mental attitude often succeed sooner or later, sometimes when they least expect it. That's why attitude plays so important a role in stand hunting for whitetails. Having a good attitude has helped me and it can help you, too.

Part of having a positive mental attitude about stand hunting is the realization that it isn't necessary to kill a deer to have a successful hunt. Many other aspects of the hunt are enjoyable, such as quality time at camp with friends and relatives and sharing experiences with others while afield.

Chapter 14

When to Hunt

Mental preoccupation with the sandwich in my backpack and a gurgling stomach were clues that it was close to lunchtime. The fact that I hadn't seen any deer since about 9:00 a.m. probably helped turn my thoughts toward nourishment, to keep me from becoming bored. A time check revealed it was 11:55 a.m.

I thought about digging the sandwich out, then decided to wait. I had seen rutting bucks during the noon hour before—often enough that I consider it a prime time to be alert, watching and listening for other bucks.

A buck was actually overdue. I had expected to see one before then because the terrain around me was littered with scrapes and rubs. The anticipated visit could come at any time, but I had a feeling it would be by 1:00 p.m., so I didn't want to be distracted by food at the moment.

It was a good thing I delayed lunch because no more than a couple of minutes went by when I heard a commotion behind me. I readied my rifle in anticipation of a shot. Not long afterward the dark brown rack of a decent buck floated into view to my left above the hazel brush, followed by the deer's head and neck. The gorgeous whitetail was swinging his head from side-to-side, as if he was looking for something.

At a distance of 16 yards it was easy to settle the cross hairs from my scope on the base of the buck's neck. When he paused for an instant I squeezed the trigger. I'll choose a beautiful 8-pointer like that one over lunch any day. If it wasn't high noon when I dropped that buck, it was darn close.

After my tag was filled, I took the time to relax and eat a sandwich. That lunch was one of the best and most memorable I've ever eaten. The remote Saskatchewan bush country and a mature buck wearing my tag added unsurpassed atmosphere and flavor.

I'm a fan of midday stand hunting for whitetails. I've shot at least as many, and perhaps more, rack bucks during hours in the middle of the day as early and late. The hour between noon and 1:00 p.m. is tops for buck sightings, especially during the rut, but any time between 10:00 a.m. and 2:00 p.m. can be good. Hunters who aren't in the field during those midday hours are missing out on some potentially hot action.

The best time to hunt whitetails from a ground blind or tree stand is any time that you can when hunting season is open. However, there are certain times of the day and the season when the chances of seeing

Many of my best bucks have been taken during the midday period. Here I am with a Saskatchewan 8-pointer I shot at noon.

deer are best. Whenever the odds of seeing whitetails goes up, so do the prospects of tagging one. Weather can play an important role in hunting success, too. Some days are better for deer hunting than others due to prevailing weather conditions.

This chapter is about those times that up your odds of ambushing a deer. The rut is the absolute best time of the year to tag a buck because antlered whitetails are more active and vulnerable then than any other time of year. It's not a bad time of year to connect on a doe, either, because their activity level also increases during the breeding season.

Although midday is prime time, any hour of the day during the rut can be terrific to intercept a buck because bucks spend so much time on the move. It's actually best to hunt all day, if you can, when the rut is on. I emphasized the value of midday hunting at the beginning of this chapter because that's when many hunters leave the woods and take a break for lunch.

The first days of any deer season, especially the first one of the year, are often among the best for hunting because a maximum number of deer are available and they aren't normally as wary as they will be later on. It's been months since they've been hunted and their guard is usually down. Heavy hunting pressure common on many opening days of gun seasons might also result in more deer activity than normal. All of those factors increase the chances for success.

Storm and cold fronts can work in a hunter's favor. Whitetails have a sixth sense that enables them to know when a storm is approaching. They are frequently busy feeding before the storm arrives and then again after it's over, especially if severe weather lasts a day or more. If the weather has been warm-to-hot for at least a week and whitetails have been primarily nocturnal to avoid the heat, a cold front can turn things around by promoting daytime activity among local deer.

I will expand on all of these other prime times to hunt, but let's finish the discussion about midday hunting. When you think about it, it makes sense that some bucks are active at midday. Those that bed down by daylight or soon afterward, roughly 7:00 a.m. where I hunt during November, have been down for five hours by noon, giving them plenty of time to rest and chew their cud. Many whitetails are ready to change positions or eat by then. In the case of bucks during the rut, they are anxious for female companionship. When hormone levels are at their peak, they may be too restless to remain inactive for more than two or three hours at a time, resulting in potential sightings by 10:00 a.m.

After a midday period of activity, bucks often bed down again until late in the day or after dark. Under those circumstances, there may actually be more buck activity during midday than early and late. Hunters who are only in the field until 9:00 or 10:00 a.m. and after 3:00 p.m. without seeing many deer might change their luck by hunting the midday period. This can be true throughout hunting seasons, not just during the rut.

I'm convinced that midday movement among whitetails is a normal part of their daily routine. It certainly was with that Saskatchewan 8-pointer because there weren't any other hunters for miles around to interrupt the local deers' normal habits. Guide Mike Aftanas and I used a 3-wheeler to travel three miles from the nearest road to reach my stand. There was no sign, audible or visible, of anyone else in the area. There was fresh snow on the ground, so the presence of any other hunters would have been easy to see.

After the buck was down, I backtracked him a short distance and discovered he had been chasing a doe. The noise of the doe running first alerted me. Her tracks revealed that she made an abrupt turn to the left (going away from me) when directly behind me. That's why I didn't see her. Fortunately for me, the buck missed the turn and ended up in my sights. The antlered whitetail was looking for the doe when I shot him.

As if that isn't enough evidence that midday is prime time for big bucks, I claimed an even bigger buck during the same time period the following year while hunting with Mike. I was in the same spot where I shot the 8-pointer, only this time I was in a tree stand rather than on the ground. The elevated position allowed me to look over the area's thick hazel brush that had temporarily blocked the previous year's buck from my view.

On the second day in the stand I dropped a 10-pointer at 10:05 a.m. Oddly enough, that whitetail had a tine growing out of the center of his skull to go with a normal 9-point rack. When taxidermist Jim Haveman from Traverse City, Michigan, mounted that deer head for me, he discovered that the tine growing from the center of the buck's skull was probably a birth defect or the result of a head injury when the whitetail was younger. He said the distance from the eye socket to the base of one antler was less than the other, which is something he hadn't seen before in the course of mounting many deer heads.

When I shot that 10-point, he was following the tracks of a doe that walked by the tree I was in the previous evening. When stand hunting keep in mind that a buck can follow the tracks of a doe you've seen at any time, including a day later.

Midday buck activity isn't limited to Canada. I caught on to the value of midday hunting while hunting in my home state of Michigan with my brother Bruce and my uncle George. To increase our chances of seeing deer, we frequently posted from daylight to dark. Over a span of years, time periods that were most productive eventually became obvious. We had our share of action early and late in the day, but midday was better by far.

Over the span of nine years that we hunted together, the three of us either killed or shot at nine bucks before 10:00 a.m., for an average of one per year. Our tally for the midday period was 16, close to a pair of sightings per year. We only shot at six bucks during evening hours (after 2:00 p.m.) over the course of those same years.

The fact that most of our posts were not near feeding areas might account for less activity during evenings than other times of day. Midday sightings were highest from stands overlooking breeding areas and security cover such as cedar swamps, balsam fir thickets and tag alder swales. However, I've seen my share of midday bucks in stands of hardwood trees, too.

We picked stand sites in locations where we expected bucks to feel secure at any time during legal shooting hours. Heavy cover represents security to a buck, whether he's checking scrapes, trying to elude a

I approach another Saskatchewan buck taken during the four hours in the middle of the day. This one has 10 points, including a tine protruding between the two main beams.

My brother Bruce with a beautiful 8-pointer he got with a muzzleloader at 1:00 p.m. during a late season hunt. He was posted along a migration trail when he connected.

hunter who jumped him or on his way to feed. The same stand we saw bucks from at midday could just as easily have been visited by a buck early in the morning or in the evening, and they sometimes were. That's why we most often posted all day.

Although I've emphasized stand hunting at midday during gun season, that is certainly not *only* the season when the advice applies. The middle of the day can also be productive for waiting out whitetails during early and late seasons, whether hunting with bow and arrow or gun. More rutting activity probably takes place during fall bow seasons than gun hunts, so the chances of catching a buck on the move during midday are at least as good then— perhaps even better.

George, Bruce and I still try to hunt all day during the rut because a buck or doe can be seen at any time. Such a strategy makes sense because the more time a hunter spends in the field, his or her chances of success increase. On days when it's not possible to hunt from dawn to dark, we try to hunt during as much of the midday period as possible.

During all day vigils we carry lunches with us. Then when hunger strikes, food is handy. I try to space the meal out during lulls in deer activity. That's easy to do most of the time since there are often hours between sightings. Pacing food consumption while on stand helps fight boredom and reduces the chances of being caught off guard.

My lunch usually contains plenty of snack foods such as cookies, granola bars, fruit and candy. Small items can be eaten quickly without much distraction. Food is wrapped in material that will be as quiet as possible when it's opened, such as cellophane. I usually cut my sandwiches in half and sometimes quarters, to reduce the size of portions I have to deal with at any one time.

I always check my surroundings carefully before eating and stay as alert as possible while eating to reduce the chances of missing a deer. I minimize my movements, too, doing every move slowly. I seldom carry any liquids with me, but a cup of hot coffee, soup or chocolate from a thermos bottle can hit the spot on cold days. Water or a soft drink can come in handy at times.

I enjoy eating lunch while afield in spite of the occasional frozen sandwich because it allows me to maximize my hunting time and to savor food that might otherwise be mundane. Wherever I happen to be in whitetail country, the setting adds its unique flavor, unsurpassed by the fanciest restaurants. I wait too long for deer season and the rut to arrive each year to leave the woods unnecessarily for a meal. Besides, there's plenty of time for eating after the sun sets.

I realize it's difficult to impossible for some hunters to remain in one place all day. It isn't necessary to do so to take advantage of midday buck activity. Still-hunting can be alternated with posting, as much to warm up and remain alert as anything else. Midday can also be a good time to try

Opening days of any deer season are always a good time to be afield. There's normally a maximum number of whitetails available, and they are often more active during hours of daylight than later on. David Miles bagged this nice 9-pointer on opening day in South Carolina while hunting from the Cedar Knoll Hunt Club.

George Smith and his son Craig drag an 8-pointer that George collected on an opening day.

rattling and deer calls, as long as you know you won't be attracting the attention of other hunters to your location. Calling or rattling could bring a rutting buck to you that might otherwise have gone unseen.

Warm fronts represent one of the worst times to hunt during midday. Temperatures that are warm to hot, such as the 70 to 80 degree range, tend to reduce midday deer activity at any time, even during the rut. The middle of the day is when temperatures are usually the highest and that's when most whitetails will be bedded in the shade. That doesn't mean no bucks will be active during midday under those conditions, but the chances of seeing them are lower than when temperatures are cool to cold.

Try to spend as much time as possible stand hunting when a cold front blows in after a warm spell. Such a change in weather often promotes increased daytime activity among whitetails. I've been lucky enough to cash in on bucks during cold fronts in Texas, Alabama and Georgia, to name a few states where a change in weather has been an important factor in hunting success.

Besides during the rut, I most like to hunt during midday when there's a full moon. Whitetails seem to be most active under the cover of darkness when the moon is full, but there will be some movement during the middle of the day. I shot two of my best whitetails during the middle of the day when the moon was full. Both bucks were bagged in Saskatchewan while I was hunting with Mike Aftanas.

My best buck was taken during the last week of the province's muzzleloader season in late October. I shot the non-typical 12-pointer with a 9-inch drop tine at 1:50 p.m., dropping it with my .50 caliber Knight Legend front loader. The antlers had a gross score of 175 6/8 and netted 165 6/8. I collected a trophy 10-pointer that netted 147 4/8 on the last day of November at 1:20 p.m. The day before I got the 10-point, I passed up a 140-class 9-pointer at 11:00 a.m.

Midday hunting can be good during late seasons, too, when temperatures are occasionally downright frigid. The middle of the day is usually the warmest under those conditions—at least that's when the thermometer readings are the highest. Deer are frequently active then, either feeding or traveling. In snow country, whitetails often move from summer to winter range once the white stuff starts accumulating. Much of this migration takes place during midday.

Opening days of deer seasons are always special, whether or not a deer is tagged. Those are the days most of us wait all year for. It's a pleasure simply to be in deer country with family and friends. Besides beginning a new season, opening days can be a great time to tag a deer. There are normally more whitetails shot on opening days than on any other day of the season, partly because deer and hunter numbers are often highest then. If you don't get a whitetail on the first day, it doesn't mean you won't score. I've shot deer on virtually every day of various seasons by being persistent and patient. You can, too.

Coincidentally, one of my first opening day bucks, a nice 6-pointer, was shot about noon. The buck was pushed into me by a hunter who had

Hunting before and after a storm can be productive. In the picture on the left I'm shown approaching the second of two bucks (an 8-pointer) I shot by 2:15 p.m. the day after a November blizzard. The first buck was a spikehorn.

left his blind and was walking out of the woods for lunch. That's another reason I like midday hunting, especially on opening days. However, I usually hunt all day on opening days, unless I connect early. Other stand hunters would be wise to do the same.

Storm fronts can be the key to deer hunting success at any time of the season, so always try to keep an eye on the weather to anticipate their arrival. The best deer hunters pay attention to weather forecasts, when possible, so they can anticipate what conditions to prepare for in terms of clothing. The day before a storm arrives and the day after are generally the best ones to hunt. However, if a storm doesn't start until afternoon, for example, it's a good idea to be on stand during the morning. When a storm breaks up part of the way through a day, get in position as soon as possible to take advantage of the deer activity that should develop.

One of the best days of deer hunting I enjoyed as a result of a storm front was the day after a blizzard ended. Heavy snow started falling on November 15th that year, which is opening day of Michigan's gun season. Deer should have been active that day, and I'm sure they were, but you couldn't prove it by me. I posted all day on the 15th without seeing a single whitetail, but a pair of hunters from another party who were hunting nearby did tag bucks that day.

The blizzard hit with full force on the 16th, with strong winds and more snow. Weather and road conditions were so bad that day that I didn't hunt. The morning of the 17th dawned clear and cold with more than a foot of new snow on the ground. I wore snowshoes to reach my post. By 2:15 p.m. on that day my season was over: I had filled both of my buck tags. I shot a spikehorn by 10:00 a.m. and my second tag went on a 3 1/2-year-old 8-pointer that followed the tracks of a doe I had seen earlier.

Heavy rains in the south can have the same impact as snowstorms in the north. An excessive accumulation of rain or snow may call for a change in areas or stand sites. Either condition can make some locations inaccessible or modify deer movements. Hunters who adapt to those changes have the best chance of seeing whitetails.

Under extreme conditions, deer may restrict movements for a day or two before a burst of activity develops. When that happens, hunters who are out there at the right time are bound to see plenty of action. Alabama deer guide Andy Dunnaway told me that a freak snowstorm developed during his state's deer season one year. Local whitetails were so shocked by the snow and cold that they didn't move for two days. He said there were tracks everywhere on the third day as whitetails resumed feeding with a vengeance.

It's great to hunt whitetails from a blind or stand anytime you can, but when you want to increase your chances of seeing deer, there are certain days that are better than others. By hunting and spending as much time in the field as you can during those days, you can up your odds of filling a tag. Whenever possible, hunt opening days, during the rut, the midday period, before and after storm fronts.

Chapter 15

Making the Shot

One of the toughest shots I have made with a rifle was responsible for me getting a big-bodied 8-pointer in Alabama during January of 1995. I was hunting with Charles Dixon of Selma out of his Bow and Gun Camp. I only had a shot at the whitetail's neck and I was using a borrowed rifle I had never fired before.

I had taken my scoped Knight muzzleloader on the hunt, but the sight got knocked off during the airplane flight there. I found out when I missed an easy 30 yard shot at a high-antlered 8-point. I should have taken a shot at a target upon my arrival, which is always a good idea when flying anywhere for a hunt, but I didn't and it cost me that deer.

Another hunter from Pennsylvania who has the same name as me, but a different middle initial (C.), had a spare .30-06 with him and he offered to let me use it. I gladly took Rick up on the offer. The rifle was a sporterized Springfield 03 that originally belonged to Rick's father. He had the barrel cut down from 26 to 20 inches and put a synthetic stock on it along with a 3-9 power scope.

Big-bodied 8-pointer I dropped in Alabama with a neck shot from a borrowed rifle. The scope of the rifle I brought with me had been knocked off during the airplane flight there.

The military trigger had a little slack in it, but not much. Although

I didn't fire a round through the rifle before hunting with it, I dry fired it once to get a feel for the trigger. The shells Rick gave me to go with the rifle were 150 grain Nosler Ballistic tip handloads. As I found out later, the combination of rifle and bullets worked fine.

It was the third day of hunting with the borrowed rifle that I had my chance at the big 8-pointer. I was in an elevated blind (locally called a shooting house) overlooking a rye grass field surrounded by thick brush that morning. It was foggy until about 9:00 a.m. As the fog was starting to clear off, I made the sound of a doe bleat with a Primos deer call and the buck appeared suddenly in the brush next to the field about 60 yards away. The rut was underway at the time and the whitetail was curious, but not curious enough to walk in the open.

The thick brush made a clear shot impossible. I could see the outline of the buck's body, but the brush was so thick I was sure a bullet would be deflected and I didn't want to risk wounding the deer. The big southern whitetail eventually walked off, but more doe bleats brought him back to the same spot minutes later. By being patient, I was eventually able to find an opening in the brush for a neck shot.

I had rested the rifle on the window sill of the blind soon after the buck reappeared, to be ready in case an opening developed. My chance came when the deer stretched his neck upward to work the branch of a pine tree above a scrape. He was standing broadside, giving me a side view of the neck. I aimed for the middle of the neck, dropping the cautious buck instantly.

Realizing that if the bullet had struck the neck anywhere other than dead center the whitetail could only be temporarily stunned, I got out of the blind immediately to follow up on the shot. I would have stayed in the blind if I could have covered the fallen deer from there, but the brush blocked it from view when it fell. When I reached a spot where I could see the buck, he was thrashing around like he was trying to get up.

He was laying on his side with the top of his back toward me, so I aimed for the center of the back between the shoulders and shot again. It's always a good idea to be ready with a second shot on deer that drop instantly. Always shoot them again if they aren't dead. I've heard too many stories from hunters who thought a whitetail was down for good when it was only stunned from a blow to the neck, spine or head. Some of those bucks got away because the hunters weren't ready with a second shot when the animals got back on their feet.

If you're able to move in close to the deer for a finishing shot, the center of the neck is an excellent place to put it. If the whitetail is moving its neck or you plan on mounting the head and don't want to damage the cape, a shot behind the shoulder will do the job. When a downed deer has its back facing you as that 8-pointer did, aim where I did.

The Alabama 8-pointer continued struggling after the second shot, so I shot a third time and that did the trick. I later found out that all three rounds had connected where they were supposed to, but it doesn't hurt to make sure a deer that's down stays there. That buck proved to be the biggest one taken by Dixon's hunters during the 1994-95 season. The heavy rack had a gross score of 130 1/8 and netted 126. The deer weighed 215 pounds in the round. For information about hunting Alabama's Black Belt with Charles Dixon contact him by writing 406 Battery Ave., Selma, AL 36701 or calling 334-875-1384.

I don't normally take neck shots or recommend them for anyone else, unless a deer is close and/or that's the only shot possible. It was obvious after watching that Alabama buck as long as I did that he wasn't likely to give me a better shot. I felt confident of making a neck shot in that case because the distance was reasonable and there was a steady rest for the rifle.

The best place to shoot a whitetail, whether hunting with gun or bow, is behind the shoulder in the middle of the body from top to bot-

WHERE TO AIM

x = Gun or Bow   + = Gun only

Whitetails that are broadside like this buck offer the best opportunity for a shot. The best point of aim is behind the shoulder in the middle of the body from top to bottom. Rifle hunters using .30 calibers or larger and shotgunners firing slugs could also aim for the center of the shoulder.

tom. Aiming for that spot insures a clean kill and allows a maximum margin for error. A bullet or broadhead that strikes a deer a few inches in any direction from the point of aim should still connect on the lungs because these vital organs take up a lot of space in the chest cavity. Whitetails seldom go far when both lungs are damaged.

Bowhunters should aim for a spot a few inches behind the shoulder to give them a margin for error in case their broadhead ends up closer to the shoulder. It's important for archers to avoid hitting the shoulder blade because this large bone can stop an arrow, usually resulting in a nonfatal hit. Since most bowhunters occupy tree stands, it's okay to aim for a point a little bit above center behind the shoulder to allow for the downward trajectory. The same is true for firearms hunters in tree stands, if the angle of the shot is steep.

Avoiding the shoulder blade isn't as critical for whitetail hunters carrying firearms that are at least .30 caliber or shotguns. Bullets of that size and slugs will go through shoulder blades, breaking them. In fact, I sometimes aim for the center of the shoulder with my .30-06. Such a hit often anchors a whitetail on the spot. Aiming for a spot directly behind the shoulder is just about as good and ruins less meat.

Rifle hunters using calibers smaller than .30, on the other hand, should be sure to avoid hitting the shoulder blade. Light bullets with high velocities may expend all of their energy on the large bone, if they hit it, and not penetrate far enough to be fatal.

Whitetails must be broadside, of course, for hunters to have the opportunity to put shots directly behind the shoulder. On deer that are angling away, the best point of aim moves

On whitetails that are angling away like this one, aim for a spot in line with the opposite shoulder, so the bullet or broadhead angles forward into the chest cavity.

Nebraska 10-pointer I took with a shot as it angled away from me.

further behind the shoulder. On animals that are angling away, try to place shots as though you are aiming for the opposite shoulder, so the bullet, slug or arrow angles forward into the chest cavity. The best point of aim on whitetails that are positioned at a sharp angle, for example, is behind the rib cage.

That's the type of shot I made on a 10-pointer taken with a .50 caliber muzzleloader in Nebraska last fall. I was in a tripod stand overlooking a dry river bottom overgrown with brush when a lone doe walked from right to left into the river bottom. She soon ran back into sight with her tail clamped against her rump and went away from me, paralleling the river bottom.

I thought a buck might be chasing her, so I gripped my rifle, ready to bring it into play if a buck followed, and one did. As soon as he appeared, I got on him with the scope. His rack looked nice and appeared to have 10 points, so I decided to take him. Since he was angling away toward where the doe had gone, I aimed behind the ribs and fired. I knew I didn't have much time to shoot before the whitetail would be

Tricky Bow Shot
Excellent for Firearms

A hit in the center of the chest or at the base of the neck of this buck will result in a clean kill.

out of sight after the doe. That's often the case.

The buck ran a short distance after the shot, but was soon down. The 240 grain, .44 caliber bullet from the muzzleloader did a super job, entering in front of the right ham and damaging the liver, lungs and heart as it angled forward.

The center of the chest or the base of the neck at the top of the chest are good points of aim on deer facing directly at you. When whitetails are angling toward you, aim for the center of the side of the chest closest to you so bullets or broadheads will angle across the chest cavity. I try to avoid frontal shots when hunting with bow and arrow because the chest is a small target and there's a lot of bone to deflect an arrow. However, each hunter will have to make that choice themselves based on the circumstances and their level of confidence in their ability. A good rule of thumb is: whenever you are in doubt about making a clean kill, don't shoot, especially if there's a chance you will get a better shot by waiting.

A hit between the hindquarters will kill a deer that is facing straight away from you, but this is not the best shot to take. It can result in loss of meat. If a whitetail has its head up, a hit in the center of the back of the neck with a bullet or slug will kill it instantly.

When looking straight down on a whitetail, I aim for the center of the back. Such a hit will break the spine and the deer won't go anywhere. Aiming left or right of center might be better for bowhunters so the broadhead goes into the chest cavity. Arrows are capable of severing a whitetail's spine when going between vertebrae, but if a broadhead doesn't hit the bone right, a nonfatal wound may result.

Refer to pictures in this chapter that help illustrate where to aim on whitetails standing in different positions.

Opportunities for shots at whitetails can come and go in a matter of seconds, so it's essential that hunters always be alert. I make it a practice to hold my gun or bow in my hands as often as possible while stand hunting, especially during prime times when the chances of seeing deer are highest. Less

Best Shot for Gun Hunter

On deer angling toward you, aim for the center of the side of the chest closest to you.

time and movement are required to take a shot when a rifle or bow is in hand, which also reduces the odds of making noise and being seen or heard.

When occupying a stand site for a long period of time, constantly gripping a gun or bow can get tiring, so I may hang it where it's handy, or lean it against a tree or the corner of a blind. However, I grab it instantly at the first hint that a deer may be nearby. Such quick action has paid off a number of times. It's always easy to put the gun or bow aside again if the sight or sound proves to be a false alarm. But if it's show time, it's better to be ready for action sooner than later.

Since whitetails can be so unpredictable, I often take the first good shot (one I know I can make) at an animal I want. I make an exception for deer that are coming toward me. I keep them covered as they approach, waiting for them to stop in an opening or to reach a point where

I know I can't miss. Then I shoot. If a deer that's getting closer suddenly becomes alert and looks like it might run or turn, I take the first good shot possible.

When bowhunting, I may never shoot at a whitetail I want, no matter how close it is, if it isn't in the right position. I seldom release an arrow at a deer unless it is broadside or angling away. Here are the best times to draw a bow for a shot at a deer: when the animal is looking away; when it is distracted by another deer or something else; when it has its head behind a tree. Those are also the best times to make

With a rifle, I would aim for the center of this buck's back near the shoulder. If I were going to take this shot with bow and arrow, I would aim to the left of the spine just in front of the clump of snow.

a move with a gun, if it isn't yet in hand or ready to shoot.

After years of hunting woodland whitetails, I've learned that the best way to connect on a buck that's walking or running is to cover an opening or shooting lane it is headed for and be ready to shoot when the sights are on its shoulder as it enters the lane. Rifle bullets are so fast that no lead is required if a deer is less than 50 yards away. When the deer is closer to 100 yards away, a little lead is a good idea. By swinging a rifle or shotgun with a whitetail in wooded habitat, there's a greater chance of hitting a tree than the deer. However, that technique can work on animals in open habitat.

The best way to connect on a moving whitetail when you are hunting wooded habitat is to take aim at an opening it is about to enter and squeeze the trigger when the sights are on target. This nice buck's shoulder will soon be in the opening where it's neck is now. You should be ready to shoot when the chest cavity gets there.

The same strategy mentioned for gun hunters applies to bow hunters when an animal is a maximum of 20 yards away. A little lead may be required, but not much. Some hunters refuse to take shots at running deer. That's fine. No one should shoot if they are unsure of making a fatal hit. Stationary whitetails certainly make better targets. Walking or running deer can sometimes be stopped by a sharp whistle. However, they may not always stop where a shot is possible. For best results, try a whistle as a moving deer is entering an opening or already in the clear.

Avoid taking a shot unless there's a clear path from your gun or bow to a whitetail. It doesn't take much of a twig to deflect an arrow, resulting in a wounding hit or a miss. And there's no such thing as a bullet or slug that plows through brush and stays on target. It doesn't

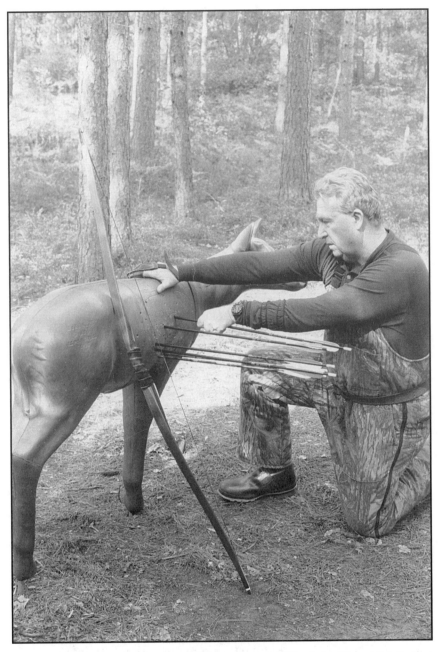

As much practice as possible is essential to prepare yourself for shots at live whitetails. Kent Horner is shown practicing with his long bow in this photograph.

take much of an opening to get a bullet or slug through, but most will be deflected when hitting brush before reaching their target, unless the obstruction is close to a deer. For best results, always wait for a white-tail to step into an opening before you take a shot.

One of the most important aspects of being able to make shots at whitetails while stand hunting with gun or bow is familiarity with your equipment. The following should all be automatic moves: raising a rifle or shotgun and getting the sights on a deer as quickly as possible, taking the safety off, reaching your anchor point when coming to full draw, releasing an arrow smoothly and squeezing the trigger. The best way for those procedures to become automatic is through lots of practice. It's impossible to practice too much.

All practice does not have to involve firing shells or arrows at the range, either. If you can only make it to the range once or twice a week, and if you hunt with a heavy bow, you should pull the string back a number of times every day. Simply drawing the bow will keep your muscles in shape or get them there. One year when I moved up to a 60 pound pull bow from a 50, the only practice I did the first few weeks was to draw the bow to get my muscles used to the heavier draw weight.

An excellent way to practice taking aim with any type of firearm is to pick out potential targets and see how fast you can steady the sights on them. This should be done with an unloaded gun. If you can continue looking at the target while bringing the gun up and if you have the sights where you want them as soon as it's up, you're ready for whitetail hunting.

To practice your trigger squeeze with an unloaded firearm, steady the sights on target and dry fire it. If the sights remain on target when the hammer falls, you are doing it right. If you flinch or jerk the trigger, the gun and sights will be moved off target. This type of practice can help cure a flinch or trigger jerking. Always wear ear protection when practicing with firearms to prevent developing a flinch. If the recoil from a rifle or shotgun is responsible for a flinch, switch to a lighter caliber or smaller gauge.

The more you practice and become proficient with firearms and/or bow and arrow, the more confidence you will have when it's time to take a shot at a deer. The more confidence you have, the less likely you are to get nervous or develop a case of buck fever. It's normal to get excited when the opportunity for a shot arrives. The better you are at handling your gun or bow, the better your chances of concentrating on making the shot and controlling the excitement until the shot has been executed. There's plenty of time for excitement after a bullet or broad-head has been put through a whitetail's chest cavity.

When occupying stands/blinds overlooking feeding areas, hunters normally have more time than usual to make shots on whitetails. Deer will often feed for at least a few minutes, and commonly much longer, before moving on. Hunters who feel a case of buck fever coming on under these circumstances should take the time to calm down before taking a shot. Taking some deep breaths and reciting some key phrases to help you concentrate on making a good shot can help.

A bowhunter may want to repeat, "Pick a spot," over and over again. Some bowhunters I know tape that slogan to their bows as a reminder, so they see the words when preparing for a shot. That's a good reminder for gun hunters to keep in mind because it's essential for all hunters to aim at a specific spot on a whitetail, not the whole deer. A phrase that would work just as well for gun hunters is, "Squeeze the trigger!"

Anything that can help you concentrate long enough to get the job done will work. Actually picking a spot visually on a whitetail's anatomy where you want to put a bullet or broadhead is a good move. It can help you concentrate on where to aim and forget about a whitetail's rack, if it happens to be a big buck. Once you've decided to shoot a buck, you should forget about its antlers. If you don't, it can distract you from making best shot possible. After all, there will be plenty of time to look at the antlers of a whitetail after it's on the ground.

Chapter 16

Mobile Stand Hunting

I was standing against a tree at the upper end of a narrow valley that funneled deer uphill from a swamp into a stand of northern hardwood trees when I heard a whitetail blow. The snort came from downhill near where the valley and swamp merged. A careful search of the area revealed a doe followed by a fawn about to enter the lower end of the valley from the swamp where a downdraft of air had carried my scent to them.

Although the doe smelled me, she was unsure where I was and milled around for five minutes or so before finally heading back in a westerly direction. The two had come from the west, but they retreated along a different course.

It was November 17th and the rut was still on, so there was a chance a buck might be trailing the doe. The fact that the deer didn't backtrack was a hint. The fawn had looked back along their backtrail a number of times, too, perhaps looking for a trailing deer.

Any buck that came along was sure to smell me like the doe had, if I remained in the same place. My vantage point also did not afford me a view of the doe and fawn as they approached. If a buck was

Leaving one stand to try another can sometimes be the best policy rather than staying put in one place. This is recommended when the wind switches or deer movements change. Some stands are also better than others at different times of the day.

following in their tracks, I wouldn't be able to see him any better. A change in positions was obviously in order.

I moved downhill to the edge of the swamp—a distance of about 75 yards—and took up a position to the right of where the doe and fawn had been. There I had a good view of their backtrail and the wind was more favorable. It was 4:30 p.m. when the doe blew. At 5:00 a whitetail appeared following their tracks. The whitetail had antlers.

Through my scope I counted six points on the buck's rack when it stopped about 50 yards away. It would have been easy to shoot that whitetail, but I was looking for something bigger, so I passed him up. If it hadn't been for mobile stand hunting, I probably wouldn't have had a chance to decide about shooting that buck. There's a good chance I might not have even seen the deer.

Mobile stand hunting has a lot of potential for whitetail hunting—whether you hunt from the ground or trees, whether you use guns or bow and arrow. The 6-pointer I passed up was the first of three bucks I could have shot while trying the method. I ended up shooting the third one, which was a respectable 8-pointer.

Traditional stand hunting generally involves remaining in a fixed position for hours at a time, watching for whitetails that wander by, anticipating that the one you want will eventually walk into shooting range. Most tree stands or ground blinds are situated where whitetails are likely to travel: feeding, bedding and breeding areas or the trails between those destinations.

Some of the best stand hunters have the patience to remain in one place all day. If necessary, they return to the same post day after day until they are successful or until their time runs out. There is certainly a time and place for that type of persistence. I've enjoyed my share of success this way. As I've become more discriminating about the bucks I shoot, however, I've discovered that being more mobile and flexible by changing stand sites regularly is often the better method.

There are good reasons for this. Wind and weather conditions frequently change from day-to-day. They sometimes undergo a dramatic transformation during the course of a day. Deer movements routinely shift in response to those changes, as well as to how much they are disturbed by hunters, what phase the rut is in and how food availability varies. Hunters who don't change stands in an effort to keep up with variable deer movements are destined to spend some boring vigils without much, if any, deer activity.

A lot of hunters don't realize how adept whitetails are at determining where and when we hunt. Deer don't have to see or smell us in a blind to identify danger zones. Based on lingering scent they can pinpoint locations with a lot of human activity during hours of darkness.

Mature bucks are usually the first animals to start avoiding stand sites, followed by does and young bucks.

Veteran deer hunter Ronnie Groom from Panama City, Florida, told me that he watched a buck that modified its route to avoid a tree stand that had been in place less than 24 hours. The day before hunting season started Groom put the stand up in a strip of trees that funneled local whitetails along a nearby creek. The stand overlooked a well-used trail.

Ronnie was in the stand with his bow the next day when he saw the buck coming on the trail. Before getting within range, the whitetail detoured from the trail to thick cover along the creek and returned to the trail after a safe distance beyond the bowhunter. Groom is convinced that the buck encountered his scent at the stand site the night before, causing him to avoid the area.

By changing stand sites and blinds regularly, hunters keep deer guessing and reduce deer's ability to avoid being seen and shot. A shift of as little as 50 to 100 yards may be enough to give you a shot at a buck that was trying to detour around your former position or that's trailing a doe that detected you. Ronnie said he seldom hunts more than a morning and evening from the same stand. He usually hunts a different stand in the evening than the one he was in during the morning. If the wind changes direction while on stand, increasing the chances deer will smell him, he moves to another position immediately where the wind will be more favorable.

Other hunters would be wise to follow his example. It helps to have a number of stands or blinds set up in advance, as Ronnie does, to allow for hunting under various wind conditions. It's easier to move when that's the case. The shift can be done as quickly and quietly as possible.

However, it isn't necessary to have blinds or stands set up in various locations to make mobile stand hunting work. When I employed the technique, I hunted from the ground and relied only on natural cover and camo clothing for concealment. A tree trunk is all that's needed to break up a hunter's outline, whether the hunter is standing or sitting. Fallen trees, bushes, brush, rocks and more can also be used as natural blinds. Adapting to changing conditions and being flexible enough to use what cover is available are a big part of what mobile stand hunting is all about.

Camo netting can be used to construct temporary ground blinds, too. Commercial blinds and stands designed to be put up and taken down quickly are also available. Veteran bowhunter Jimmy Dean is one of the best mobile stand hunters I've interviewed. He uses a tree sling and tree steps to move from stand to stand.

It isn't necessary to have blinds or stands set up in various locations to take advantage of mobile stand hunting. I normally use natural cover as much as possible, as this hunter is doing.

A stand site that wasn't as good as I expected it to be got me started on mobile stand hunting. The spot was a prime breeding area that had produced two bucks for me on previous hunts. However, there had been no snow on the ground when I scored there. An out-of-state hunt prevented me from scouting the area for fresh activity before the season opened. When I arrived at my hot spot on opening day there was snow on the ground and little or no sign of fresh activity.

The terrain was basically flat where the breeding area was, but a high ridge I descended to get there wasn't far away. By backtracking to the top of the ridge, I found that I could watch the breeding area and terrain on top of the ridge where there had been some recent deer activity. That's where I decided to post. I stayed put all day.

I saw three deer on top of the ridge. A doe and fawn appeared first about 100 yards away. There were a lot of saplings between us, making it impossible to shoot at any buck that might come along behind them. I thought about moving closer to where they had been to be prepared in case a buck came along later, but I didn't act on the thought.

About half an hour later a buck did show up following the doe. It was a yearling with small antlers that I wasn't interested in shooting. However, that animal could have just as easily been a wallhanger. By not taking the initiative to change positions, I missed an opportunity. The lesson sunk in.

Although I only saw the three deer, I heard a fourth late in the day. The snow was crunchy, making it easy to hear its footsteps in an area where a group of evergreen trees blocked my view. I tried grunting and rattling to lure the deer into view, but got no response.

After dark I checked out the unseen deer's tracks by flashlight. I discovered its trail crossed those of the three deer I had seen. I put that information to good use the next day by posting in a new spot about 100 yards to the west of where I had been the day before. The new vantage point provided me a good opportunity for a shot at any deer that traveled where any of the whitetails had the day before. I could no longer see the breeding area, but there hadn't been any recent movement there anyway.

The wind shifted during the course of the day, so I adjusted positions once more, going further west. My next stand was at the upper end of the narrow valley that angled downhill to the swamp. The three whitetails I saw the day before walked up that valley. The one I heard had walked by within view of the new spot where I posted, giving me just as good coverage as I had at the previous location.

I was at stand number three when the doe winded me. Another move allowed me to get the drop on the 6-pointer. I think the doe and fawn were the same ones I had seen the day before, but the buck was bigger. Over the course of two days I had occupied four stand sites before getting a good chance at a buck. The moves, none of which were a distance of more than 100 yards, helped me fine tune my positioning. The same process continued the next day I hunted.

A couple of days elapsed before I returned to the area to resume hunting. The weather had warmed during that interval, melting a lot of snow. I planned on posting on the north side of the narrow valley again, but the wind was wrong, so I ended up in a new spot on the south side. I was at a high point even with the middle of the valley.

Soon after daylight a deer entered the valley from the north slope. It proved to be a 3-pointer that would have been easy to shoot, but I let it go. I think it was the yearling I saw trailing the doe and fawn on opening day. The buck moved up the valley and soon went out of sight. It hadn't been gone from view more than a minute when a second deer that was larger appeared at the top of the valley on the north side and trotted after the 3-pointer. It wasn't in view long enough for me to tell if there were antlers on its head.

On the chance I could get a better look, I moved to the upper end of the valley as quickly and quietly as I could. The deer was gone by the time I reached a point where I could see the terrain where it went. I ended up staying at the upper end of the valley where visibility was better than where I had been.

By midday I had seen four more deer: a pair of does that each had a fawn. Soon afterward, curiosity about any new developments at the breeding area got the best of me. The 3-pointer and the unidentified animal were headed that way. I thought activity might have increased there with the decrease in snow cover.

A visit to the spot confirmed that was the case. There were four or five super-fresh scrapes present, including a huge one under the

I shot this mature 8-pointer while I was mobile stand hunting. I connected on the whitetail after moving to a stand overlooking fresh scrapes.

My brother Bruce and I drag the buck I took while mobile stand hunting past a pair of fresh scrapes that helped me decide to post nearby.

branches of a large balsam fir tree. Fresh, jumbo deer tracks criss-crossed the area.

At about 2:30 p.m. I got in position at a stand overlooking the fresh scrapes. An hour had almost elapsed when a hot doe accompanied by a mature buck approached the scrapes. As soon as I saw the buck's rack

The author hunted this area three days, relocating his stand site seven times before killing an 8-point buck late in the afternoon on the final day.

This photo shows the Montana 9-pointer I tagged after moving to a new spot. Seeing a doe being chased by a buck was responsible for me relocating. The buck doing the chasing was a spikehorn, but the bigger buck eventually showed up to try to get in on the action.

I knew it was a keeper. The beams were long and heavy, and wider than the buck's ears.

The antlered whitetail finally moved into an opening near the large scrape. That's where I shot him. One of the 8-pointer's beams was broken near the tip, but he was still a fine trophy. He proved to be 4 1/2 or 5 1/2 years old.

I ended up filling my tag from the stand site I originally planned on hunting opening day. If I would have hunted there regardless of the lack of fresh sign and stuck it out day-after-day, the outcome might not have been the same. The constant presence of my scent there might have caused the buck to establish scrapes elsewhere or made him nocturnal.

Even if I would have eventually gotten the same buck by stubbornly staying with the one stand site, there's a good possibility I wouldn't have seen the other two bucks I saw by changing stands, depriving me of the chance to fill a tag earlier if I had been willing to settle for a smaller buck. And I most certainly would not have learned as much about deer movement in adjoining country as I did by being mobile. There's no question in my mind that moving around was the best strategy under the circumstances. I plan to do it more in the future. Other hunters might be able to improve their success in the same way.

Although I occupied a total of seven different stand sites over the course of three days, changing positions as often isn't necessary to cash in on this variation of stand hunting. Changing spots once or twice may be all that's necessary to succeed, especially if you are already familiar with deer movements and terrain where you're hunting. What's necessary to make this technique work is the willingness to move where your chances of seeing deer are better. Deer sightings and the presence of fresh sign help you determine the better spot.

A number of years ago I tagged a 9-pointer in Montana by changing stands at the right time to the right place. I had seen the buck one day and selected a stand the following day where I thought I might see him again. I posted on the ground along a long, narrow opening surrounded by brush. Sign indicated deer crossed the opening in various places.

I saw plenty of does during the course of the day, but no bucks. Late in the day I saw a doe being chased by a buck along the edge of the opening about 100 yards away. When the two disappeared in the brush I hustled to a point opposite where they were last. They reappeared minutes later, but the buck was a spikehorn.

Figuring the larger buck was sure to be attracted to a hot doe, I waited. The two deer disappeared in the brush once more. Minutes later they came racing back in the open with the 9-pointer right behind them.

Whenever moving from one stand to another, you should be alert to any deer that might be encountered along the way. This is especially true when you are trying to close in on breeding activity, as I was in Montana. Bucks attracted by the presence of a hot doe can be anywhere in the vicinity. Even when no deer are in sight, bucks can be encountered anywhere at any time in the field during shooting hours. So you should always be ready.

Chapter 17

Hunting in the Rain

Sometimes it's best not to have enough sense to come in out of the rain, especially if you're interested in seeing whitetail bucks. I proved it on November 20th one year.

I was hunting a remote area of Michigan's Upper Peninsula where snow is more common than rain after gun season opens on November 15th. There was already about a foot of snow on the ground, and plenty of the white stuff clung to trees. A warm front arrived (temperatures might have reached 40 degrees Fahrenheit) along with rain. I was camping and was prepared for the snow and cold, but not rain.

I was determined to hunt anyway due to a strong feeling that the change in weather might change my luck. The area I was hunting had a low deer density, averaging 10 or less per square mile. I was there for the few trophy whitetails I knew were in the area. After four days of hunting, I had only seen one doe.

Soon after daylight on that rainy day I reached a knoll overlooking a location where I had seen the most deer sign. The first thing I did before loading my Remington Model 700 .30-06 was to dry it and the 3x-9x Bushnell scope as thoroughly as possible. The rifle bolt was in my hands when I saw the flash of a deer below me about 40 yards away. It obviously saw me move and it spooked. The animal appeared to be a small doe, but if she had a buck trailing her, he was gone, too.

Despite the fact I blew what could have been quick action, seeing that deer was a good sign. Perhaps the rain would increase daytime activity among local whitetails. I would be ready in case it did. One hour and forty minutes later I saw a second whitetail, and it was a buck.

The whitetail wasn't the one I wanted, though. It only had spikes for antlers. While bowhunting more than a month earlier a friend of mine had seen an 8-pointer in the area. I figured it was responsible for the scrapes and rubs I had seen. Even though I wasn't interested in shooting the buck in front of me, the sighting encouraged me nonetheless. It gave me hope that I might see the bigger buck, if I stuck it out.

Sticking it out proved to be a real test. I was wearing outer layers made of Polar Tuff material in a Realtree grey leaf camo pattern. Although the material is water resistant, it isn't designed to keep a person dry during long exposure to rain. I had long underwear tops and bottoms on, along with a shirt and sweatshirt. I had worn the same garments in the rain before without any discomfort, but never for an entire day and never under conditions that were as wet.

Rain fell steadily. To make matters worse, melting snow was also falling on me. I was standing against the trunk of a large evergreen tree. The tree's branches formed a canopy that would have normally offered some protection from the rain. On that day those branches were loaded with snow in meltdown. The meltdown increased rather than decreased the amount of water falling on me. It wasn't any dryer anywhere else, except in my tent, and I knew there wasn't much chance of seeing deer from there.

While hunting in the rain I passed up a spikehorn like this one. Seeing the yearling buck boosted my spirits and gave me the incentive to continue hunting, hoping to see a larger buck that I knew was in the area.

My desire to stay put all day in spite of the rain wasn't really tested until afternoon. My spirits had gotten another boost at noon when I caught a glimpse of one of two deer that approached from behind. They winded me and blew before bolting. The deer I saw was a doe.

The rain intensified during the afternoon. I got wetter and wetter as the rain and melting snow soaked through my outer layers. I eventually got cold. By 3:00 p.m. I figured I had suffered enough. It's a good thing I decided to call it a day. The walk warmed me up and reconfirmed what I already knew: the deer were active in the rain.

I counted six fresh sets of deer tracks in about a quarter mile. One of the sets of prints were big. They were probably those of a mature buck. That short walk helped me resolve to stick it out after all. Memories of big bucks that had been bagged in the rain helped a lot, too. One of the bucks that gave me the incentive to turn back was an 11-pointer I had taken in Georgia about two weeks earlier while hunting out of Calloway Gardens with Bill Jordan, Realtree camo designer and president of the company.

Remembering bucks that I knew had been shot in the rain helped me hang in there when the going got tough. One of those bucks was an 11-pointer I had taken myself in Georgia two weeks earlier. This picture shows me approaching that buck where he fell.

The circumstances were much different on that hunt. The weather was hot instead of cold. Temperatures reached the 80s on the first day. Buck sign associated with the rut such as scrapes and rubs were present, but a lot of the activity was nocturnal. We were hoping for a cold front to encourage daytime activity.

It's not that we weren't seeing bucks. We were, but not the big ones. Whitetails are far more abundant on Calloway Gardens property than where I was hunting in Michigan, but big bucks are hard to come by, wherever they live. The right weather conditions at the right time of year can sometimes make the difference.

One of the best bucks Bill Jordan has shot while hunting in the rain is this long-tined 8-pointer. It was pouring rain when he shot this whitetail.

The stand that Jordan had put me in was a big buck hot spot. A 10-pointer had been taken from the ladder stand the previous week. The year before, a pair of 9-pointers had been bagged from that perch. Plenty of other bucks were seen there, at least one of which was bigger than those that were shot.

On the first morning of my Georgia hunt I saw three different spikehorns from the stand. I watched one rub his antlers on a sapling 20 yards away. My host assured me bigger bucks were in the area and I had a good chance of seeing one, if I was patient and the weather changed.

A cold front didn't develop, but rain did by the third morning. That's when I got the 11-pointer. He appeared at 8:50 a.m., heading from a creek bottom toward some scrapes. His antlers grossed 134 2/8 and netted 127 5/8, making him one of my better whitetails.

Due to the rain, Jordan had given me a portable canopy to put above the stand that morning. A screw-in attachment made the lightweight roof quick and easy to install on the tree above me. I stayed dry during the two hours I sat in the stand due to that handy product.

As a fan of hunting in the rain, Bill Jordan is normally prepared for wet weather. He wears a two-piece, Gore-Tex rain suit when necessary. Prior to acquiring the portable canopies to keep tree stands dry in the rain, he used to secure an umbrella above his stand to fend off precipitation.

Bill has seen a lot of bucks while hunting in the rain. One of the biggest was a huge 8-pointer he bagged during the fall of 1990. The antlers from that long-tined buck scored in the 150s. It was the second best whitetail to his credit at the time.

That was one of the bucks that flashed through my mind as I turned back toward the soggy stand in Michigan that I had temporarily abandoned. The third buck that revitalized my interest in hunting in the rain that day was a Boone and Crockett qualifying 12-pointer shot by Louis Roy from L'anse, Michigan, in 1987. Louis told me that it was pouring rain when he got up on the second day of gun season that year and he had thought about going back to bed, but he resisted the temptation.

Rain gear kept him dry on the seven mile 3-wheeler ride to his remote blind. The enclosed blind he built at the site kept him dry once he got there, but he didn't have to worry about staying dry long. The

Louis Roy with the head and cape of the Boone and Crockett buck he bagged on a rainy day. This whitetail's rack is one of the highest scoring typicals on record for Michigan. The thoughts of seeing a buck like this can be inspirational.

record book buck appeared at 8:00 a.m. The impressive antlers had a final net score of 184 7/8. They rank as the second highest scoring typical rack ever bagged in the Upper Peninsula, according to state records maintained by Commemorative Bucks of Michigan.

Visions of seeing a similar buck flashed through my mind when I returned to the spot I had occupied since daylight. I knew it could happen. Although the chances of seeing a Boone and Crockett buck weren't high, the odds of getting a look at that 8-pointer my buddy had seen earlier were realistic.

The second buck I saw toward the end of a rainy day wasn't as big as I hoped to see, but I knew I had a chance at another buck by sticking it out rather than letting the wet conditions get the best of me.

Only a matter of minutes of daylight remained on that dreary day when a deer suddenly came running off of a ridge 75 yards away. It was a doe and she was soon followed by a buck. The pair danced around in front of me long enough for me to make out good forks on each of the buck's antlers. I couldn't see brow tines, but I assumed they were there, making him a 6-pointer.

I was tempted to shoot, but I didn't because he wasn't the one I wanted. Simply seeing another buck was reward enough. Sticking it out despite the rain and cold had paid off.

If anyone had seen me walking out of the woods that night, they probably would have thought I was miserable. They would have been wrong. I felt a deep-seated sense of satisfaction, bordering on euphoria, from what I considered to be a very successful day in the deer woods. The fact that I had almost let myself give in to the elements made that second buck sighting extra special. I hadn't let the weather deprive me of the high point of the day.

Of course, it would have been *more* satisfying if that buck had been an 8-point or better and I could have filled my tag. However, I felt so good because, based on years of experience as well as current conditions, I had made a move that gave me a chance at a whitetail buck. The fact that I didn't shoot the animal was less important than the fact that

I could have. Even though the buck I saw that time was a young one, I knew it could just as easily have been a keeper and possibly one for the record books.

It's not often that everything goes according to plan when hunting whitetails. The times when almost all of the elements fall into place, especially in the face of adversity, are well worth savoring. As it turned out, that rainy day was the best of the season for me in Michigan that fall. I saw five out of a possible six deer that wandered within view of my stand. Two of them were legal bucks and I could have shot both of them, which is excellent for the area I was in. The only thing I wish had been different is that I would have had rain gear with me that day.

I normally carry a poncho in my backpack while deer hunting, but I had taken it out for that hunt because the probability for rain had seemed low. I'll know better next time. When I do use a poncho, I drape it over limbs above me to form a roof, when that option is possible.

As I found out in Georgia, hunting in the rain does not have to be uncomfortable or a test of staying power. Those who go prepared for hunting in the rain can remain warm and dry at the same time they enjoy action from whitetails. As a general rule, hunters tend to be more alert to what's happening around them when they are comfortable.

Any discomfort I suffered on that memorable day in Michigan was my fault for not being prepared. Even so, if the trees in the area hadn't been covered with snow, there's a good chance I could have gotten by without getting very wet. Unburdened evergreen boughs can absorb a lot of moisture. If you should encounter the same conditions that I did, be sure you go prepared for the worst.

Full rain suits will keep you dryer than a poncho. I dislike that some rainwear is made from material that makes noise when you move, which can spook deer. However, the newer Gore-Tex suits aren't as noisy as other types. Also, when it's raining, there's often enough noise to cover sounds from a rain suit. When it's raining hard, staying dry and comfortable can be more important for you than worrying about noise, anyway, as I found out on that Michigan hunt. One way to minimize noise from rain gear is to wear it under your normal outer layers. This may be necessary to meet clothing color requirements during gun hunts in some states, if your rain suit is made of camouflaged material.

A good blind with a roof can do a superb job of keeping hunters dry, too. If you have access to such a blind, noisy rainwear won't be much of a concern. It can be taken off once inside.

If you're properly prepared, it makes sense not to come in out of the rain when you are deer hunting. Hunting in the rain may help you bag a buck for the books. More likely, the practice will provide you an opportunity at a buck that you might not otherwise have had.

Chapter 18

Bait Hunting

Baiting is a hunting method usually associated with black bear, but it also works on whitetails. Where the practice is legal, in at least 26 states and provinces, it could help you fill a tag. If nothing else, the method might improve your chances of seeing deer. That helps make hunts satisfying, even if your tag goes unfilled.

This tactic is simply a variation of hunting feeding areas. Instead of relying on a food source that might already be present such as acorns or a farm field, the hunter puts food out that attracts whitetails such as apples or corn. Once deer start visiting the feeding area, an ambush can be planned. There are definite advantages for bowhunters who use bait: shots are often taken at known distances and it's possible for feeding deer to offer the best shot, increasing the chances for clean kills.

However, when it comes to hunting whitetails, whether at bait sites or natural feeding areas, the best laid plans don't always

Apples are one of the most popular deer baits in Michigan. Bait hunting is little different than hunting other types of feeding areas, except the hunter provides the food. Contrary to popular perception, success while hunting over bait is far from guaranteed as I found out during my first attempt.

work. Regardless of how these abundant big game animals are hunted, success is never guaranteed. There's more involved in making baiting work for you than simply supplying food that deer want to eat. I found that out many years ago during my first attempt at hunting deer over bait.

My home state of Michigan is on the list of states where bait hunting is legal. I had heard about other bowhunters who had used the method successfully, so I decided to try it. I carried apples in a backpack to a remote clearing created by a forest fire years earlier. Based on past experience, I knew there were big bucks in the area and there had been no bowhunting pressure. The apples were placed in the clearing where local deer were already feeding on grass and other vegetation, so it didn't take long for them to find the food.

Deer ate the apples as fast as I put them out. After feeding the whitetails for a couple of weeks I figured it was time to fill my tag. Was I in for a surprise. Dreams of bagging a trophy buck over bait were soon forgotten. I hunted the site for several days and I did not see a single whitetail of either sex.

It didn't take long to figure out all feeding activity took place under the cover of darkness. Each morning the apples I put out the day before would be gone. I never saw anything in the evening when I waited until it got dark. Just like any hunting technique, there are ways that work and ways that don't.

I now know what I should have done differently. Instead of putting the bait in a clearing where whitetails feel uncomfortable during hours of daylight, especially when human scent is associated with the location, I should have placed it along the edge of security cover where the animals would feel comfortable feeding. Although this is true for whitetails in general, when bucks are involved, it deserves even more consideration.

Bait placement will have a major bearing on deer sightings, according to my friend Allan Koski, who has done well while bowhunting over bait. He's taken 10 bucks and two does, averaging a deer per year over a dozen years. He had an exceptional year during the fall of 1990. He missed a spikehorn on opening day of the bow season (October 1), bagged a 2 1/2-year-old 7-pointer a couple of days later and filled his second tag with a forkhorn on October 11.

Koski does a lot of scouting during both spring and fall to locate spots for placing bait. He likes to put food near existing deer trails where buck sign is present. Swamp edges are preferred bait sites.

"I like to pick spots where cover is thick," he said. "Lots of times I can only see 20 or 30 yards."

The final criteria Koski considers when selecting a bait site is a tree for a portable stand. He usually puts bait about 15 yards from the tree he plans to hunt from. Food is positioned upwind from where he will be waiting, based on prevailing wind directions.

Rather than putting all of his faith in one spot, Al normally baits three locations to prepare for changing wind directions and corresponding variations in deer movements. If conditions aren't right at one location, he's got two backups to rely on. Preparation of three sites helps protect against over-hunting one spot, too.

Too much pressure at one location may cause bucks to change feeding locations entirely. At the very least, they may revert to nocturnal feeding. If a deer detects through scent, sound or sight a hunt-

Putting bait in or near thick cover, as Sam Grissom is doing here, increases the chances of seeing deer that are taking advantage of the feed during shooting hours. Oats mixed with dry molasses are being used as bait in this case.

er who is hunting over bait, that stand should be rested for a minimum of two or three days. More often than its hearing and sight, a whitetail's sense of smell allows it to pinpoint hunters; so you should avoid hunting when wind conditions are unfavorable.

When you are deer hunting on public property, it is doubly important to maintain alternate spots, on the chance other hunters will post too close to your preferred stand. Each hunter has an equal right to use public land as they see fit, within the law. If the presence of other hunters interferes with deer movements at one location, moving to a backup stand can save the day. Competition is a fact of life on state and federal land. A couple of ways to reduce competition, if not avoid it, are either

Allan Koski with a 7-point buck he bagged while hunting over bait with bow and arrow.

to hunt further from roads than anyone else or to do most of your hunting on week days when most other hunters will probably be working.

Aerial photographs have helped Al pinpoint the best spots to hunt over bait during recent years. He obtained them from the U.S. Department of Agriculture, Agricultural Stabilization and Conservation Service, 2222 West, 2300 South, P.O. Box 30010, Salt Lake City, Utah 84130 (801-524-5856). To obtain photos of the right area, he sent a map with his hunting area outlined.

The photos enable Al to pinpoint funnels, points of upland that extend into swamps and islands of upland surrounded by swamp. Even deer trails are visible on some aerial photos.

Aerial photographs and maps can be a big help in selecting potential stand sites, whether or not you plan on using bait.

"The photos showed me all kinds of neat places to investigate," he said. "After I got an aerial photo I was able to understand my hunting area for the first time."

Al likes to move around and try new spots from year-to-year as well as during the same season. Aerial photos tip him off to plenty of places to investigate. He may not hunt three new bait sites each year, but he likes to have at least one new spot to try per year. By the time bow season ends, he usually knows where he will be hunting the following year.

One of the most important lessons Al learned about placing bait during his years of hunting is it's tough to outcompete an abundant source of natural food that deer prefer.

"I remember one year I had a tree stand among oak trees that produced a lot of acorns," Koski said.

Baiting is least effective in areas with abundant natural foods such as acorns or agricultural fields.

"My apple pile kept getting bigger as I added to it each time I hunted because the deer weren't eating them. They were passing them up for the acorns. It was real frustrating because I would watch them eating acorns for up to an hour at a distance of 40 to 50 yards, and they stayed out of bow range."

The same thing would probably happen where agricultural crops favored by whitetail, such as corn and beans, are abundant. Under those circumstances, baiting would be of little advantage. Baiting is most effective in big woods where favored deer foods are scattered or nonexistent. A study in Texas, another state where deer hunting over bait is legal, found that baiting is most effective during years when there are poor to nonexistent acorn crops.

A report on the study stated that large areas of Texas have over-populations of deer. It concluded, "considering the higher harvest rates over baited sites, baiting appears to serve as a tool for increasing the harvest of deer in areas where higher success rates are needed."

Deer densities tend to be low in big woods country. The animals can be tough to find because they are scattered over a large area. Bait can improve the odds for success by attracting to the food some deer that might not otherwise be seen.

Al relies on apples as the primary type of bait to attract deer to his stands. The fruit is a popular choice as bait throughout Michigan because many apple trees are in the wild. Koski mixes some whole kernel corn with the apples. Because kernels of corn are also attractive to birds, Al tries to cover the grain with apples when putting them on the ground.

Carrots and sugar beets are popular deer baits in Michigan's northern Lower Peninsula, but their attractiveness to whitetails varies by region. Al does his hunting in the Upper Peninsula and he tried carrots one year. The deer ignored them.

Other foods used to attract deer to stand sites are potatoes, grains such as oats and barley, cabbage, lettuce, hay, mangoes and pumpkins. Bait can be purchased from farmers and retail outlets, but Al gets satisfaction from picking his own from apple trees in the woods. He starts collecting apples during August even though some of them may be green. The apples are stored in a shed where it's cool and the fruit ripens.

Al starts putting apples and corn at bait sites during the first week of September, usually around Labor Day, which is about three weeks before bow deer season begins. Baiting is done on weekends at first, then at two or three-day intervals as opening day approaches. Twenty to 30 apples and a scoop of corn are put out per trip. Some of the apples are sliced open to allow better scent dispersal.

Prebaiting a stand site for one or two weeks before hunting is often enough time, especially when a location is selected where deer activity already exists. The first time Al tried bowhunting over bait, he only put food out for 1 1/2 weeks before starting to hunt. He arrowed a spikehorn at the end of his second day of hunting that year.

It's important to use food items local deer are familiar with and that they prefer to eat. Unfamiliar foods may be ignored, as were those carrots that Al used one year. Some states may restrict the types of bait and/or quantities that can be used for deer hunting, so be sure to check local regulations—first to see if the practice is legal, and second to see if there are any restrictions on its use where legal. Wisconsin, for example, limits the quantity of bait that can be put in the field at one time to 10 gallons.

A list of many of the states and provinces where deer hunting with bait is legal, according to local hunters and/or state wildlife officials, accompanies this chapter. There may have been changes since this list was compiled. Specific information on baiting was not available from all states and provinces.

Once Al starts hunting, he replenishes the bait supply as needed. Whitetails may visit a bait at any time of day, so Koski hunts as much as possible. When he can, he posts during mornings and evenings. He sits from daylight until 10:00 or 11:00 a.m. and then from 3:00 p.m. until dark. Most, but not all, feeding activity is in the evening.

Philbert Leonard holds up the head of a trophy buck he bagged with bow and arrow while stand hunting over bait. The 18-point non-typical was arrowed on October 14th from a tree stand. The antlers scored 175 2/8 and the buck had a dressed weight of 234 pounds.

When you are bait hunting during the rut, you'll find that morning and midday are the most productive times. Bucks will end up at baits then, as they follow does in heat or does about to come into estrus. They may follow the tracks of a doe that has already fed and gone. Bucks seen at baits during the rut are primarily interested in does rather than food, so archers should be ready to take the first good shot they are offered.

Whitetails tend to make more use of bait after the first significant snow fall when other types of food they normally feed on have been covered with snow. This buck is eating corn.

Mature bucks are most vulnerable to hunters during the rut, regardless of which hunting method is used. Hunting over bait is no different. Does that are eating the food you put out basically serve as bait to attract bucks.

Although mature bucks are most often seen at baits during the rut, they are also sometimes taken early in the season before the rut begins and during late season after the rut has ended, when they are actively feeding. Philbert Leonard from St. Ignace, Michigan, for example, bow bagged a trophy 18-point non-typical on October 14th one fall as it fed on apples he put near his stand. That big buck had a dressed weight of 234 pounds and the antlers scored 175 2/8.

Leonard got the buck at 6:30 p.m. The day he scored was the first time he hunted that year. On top of that, the buck was the first whitetail he collected with bow and arrow.

Brian Haralson from Lake Linden, Michigan, took a beautiful 9-pointer that green scored 137 on January 1 one year, which was the last day of the state's bow season. Haralson saw the buck at his bait on December 18th, but it didn't give him a good bow shot then. By being persistent and sticking it out to the very end, he finally got the trophy animal.

According to Al's experience, utilization of bait by deer increases after the first significant snowfall. Whitetails will continue feeding on bait as snow depth increases and covers some of the natural foods that the animals relied on before.

Although Al and many other hunters who use bait prefer to hunt from stands overlooking the food source, posting along runways leading to and from bait can also be productive. This is obviously the best approach in situations when most, if not all, feeding activity is nocturnal. Whitetails can sometimes be ambushed during legal shooting hours along trails as little as 50 to 100 yards from baits. However, the closer you can get to bedding areas without spooking deer, the better your chances of seeing deer before dark.

Al doesn't use scents, calls or rattling antlers to increase his chances of success while hunting over bait, but these accessories can make a difference when used properly under the right circumstances. A buck that's hesitant about approaching a bait, for example, might be enticed into bow range with a grunt tube or some sex scent.

Although my first experience with deer hunting over bait was a bust, I've tried it on a number of other occasions since then when bait was better placed and whitetails were more cooperative. The tactic has helped me fill a few tags with does and young bucks and will probably help me bag more whitetails in the future. Even when I haven't scored, I've enjoyed watching deer that visited the bait. That's a big part of what bowhunting is all about.

Here's how Al feels about deer hunting over bait: "For every deer I shoot, I've probably fed another 25 at one time or another during the season. So I am helping the rest of the herd stay healthy and hopefully better survive the winter. Knowing that I am helping many more deer than I harvest, makes me feel good."

Although deer hunting over bait can be effective when done properly, so can any other method available to hunters. Nonetheless, the effectiveness of bait hunting is sometimes overrated to the point it is labeled as unsportsmanlike and/or unethical. Based on personal experience and the experience of other bowhunters who have tried the method, I believe these accusations are false. Surveys dealing with deer hunting success with bait conducted by the Michigan Department of Natural Resources (DNR) clearly confirm that the technique is neither unsportsmanlike or unethical.

The DNR surveys dealing with deer hunting over bait were conducted in 1984 and 1991. One of the conclusions from the 1984 survey was, "Baiting had little impact on harvest, about the same number of deer were tagged/100 days with and without the use of bait. About 2.4 deer were taken over bait per 100 days of effort, compared to 2.2 taken without bait."

Baiters claimed 3.8 deer per 100 days of hunting in 1991 and non-baiters bagged 3.1 deer for every 100 days of effort, according to survey results. That means baiters invested an average of 26.3 days for every deer taken while nonbaiters scored after every 32.25 days. If we convert

Surveys done by the Michigan Department of Natural Resources confirm that bait hunting is not as effective as many people think it is. Bait hunting success is little different than other hunting methods. Baits are most often visited by antlerless deer like this one. For that reason, the method can help increase the harvest of does and fawns where needed.

the data from 1984 in the same way, we see that baiters accumulated 41.6 days for every deer taken and nonbaiters spent 45.45 days to get a deer.

A larger deer population in 1991 than 1984 resulted in better success for all hunters that year. The two reasons that baiters had a higher rate of success than hunters using other techniques during 1991 are, first, there was a poor to nonexistent acorn crop and, second, winter weather started earlier than normal, making baiting more effective. There was a good acorn crop during 1984.

Regardless, any technique that requires the investment of an average of 26.3 days of effort for every whitetail that's taken can hardly be described as unsportsmanlike or unethical, and that's under ideal conditions. Success rates were determined for all Michigan deer hunters.

If bowhunters were considered separately, they would certainly have a lower rate of success than listed above for either year.

Since gun deer season only lasts 14 days in Michigan and the majority of hunters only hunt half of the available days or less, it's easy to see that plenty of hunters could have spent all of their time afield hunting over bait and still have not gotten a deer. In fact, a lot of hunters could have spent the entire season hunting over bait and not filled a tag. Only about 25 percent of the state's deer hunters manage to tag a whitetail annually, which means 75 percent fail to use their tags, many of whom hunt over bait.

Deer hunting over bait is not for everyone. After all, it involves a lot more work than other more traditional tactics. Hunting a natural food source is certainly easier than carrying deer food afield on a regular basis. Where baiting is legal, it's simply an option for those who choose to use it. The technique may help you fill a tag, but then again, it may not. There's no guarantee of success with *any* method. Baiting is no exception.

Nonetheless, serious discussion about limiting and possibly eliminating bait hunting for deer took place in Michigan during 1995. A series of public hearings were held by the Department of Natural Resources across the state to determine what to do. The majority of Michigan residents who expressed their opinions at the hearings supported leaving the practice as is, according to DNR figures. At the hearings a total of 2,772 people took the time to express how they felt. The results were 2,182 people or 78.7 percent in favor of the method and 590 or 21.3 percent against.

Among those who would like to see baiting continue as a legal method of deer hunting, 518 or 18.6 percent would like to have some restrictions adopted. There are presently no laws governing bait hunting for deer in Michigan. Sixty percent of those who expressed their views (1,664 people) did not want any changes in current deer hunting laws.

Coincidentally, the results of a poll on deer baiting conducted by the producer of a weekly outdoor television show in Marquette had a similar response to the statewide public hearings during the course of one evening. The public hearings took place over a period of months. The number of people who expressed their opinion was almost the same, and the percentage of respondents who wanted to see no change was identical.

A total of 2,738 people called in response to a poll about baiting conducted by Buck LeVasseur on his weekly outdoor television show called "Discovering," which is aired on Marquette's WLUC-TV on Monday evenings at 7:30 p.m. Viewers were asked to choose whether they would like to see bait hunting for deer banned, quantity restrictions established or no changes made. The majority (60 percent) voted for no change in baiting regulations. Twenty-eight percent supported a quantity restriction and 12 percent favored a ban on the hunting method.

Based on the input at public hearings, no changes were made in restrictions on deer baiting in Michigan through 1996.

States Where Deer Hunting with Bait Is Legal

Arkansas	Ohio	Florida
Kansas	Oklahoma	Kentucky
South Carolina	Washington	Maryland
Texas	New Hampshire	Vermont
Michigan	Wisconsin	Montana
West Virginia	North Carolina	Louisiana
Nebraska	New Jersey	North Dakota

Provinces

New Brunswick	Ontario	Saskatchewan
Nova Scotia	Quebec	

Chapter 19

The Hofmann Buck

On November 10, 1994, Fred Hofmann from Antigo, Wisconsin, arrowed a new state record buck with typical antlers. He was using bait at the time he scored, although it played a small part in his success on the tremendous buck. This is the story of his memorable hunt.

One night during late August of 1994, hunting partners Fred Hofmann and Bill Burkhart from Bryant were shining deer in Langlade County when they saw the eyes of a deer in the road ahead of them. As they came to a stop where the whitetail had been, Hofmann heard the animal crashing through the woods as it ran off. Even though they knew the deer was gone, Burkhart turned the spotlight on for a look around.

Nothing was visible in front of them or to the left. Then Bill shined the light to the right. Both men were shocked by what the beam illuminated 10 yards from the road in a ditch. It was the biggest buck in velvet either of them had seen, with a fully developed set of antlers.

"I will never forget that sight," Hofmann said. "It was unbelievable. The buck froze for four or five seconds and then walked off into the brush."

They both agreed that the rack on that whitetail's head was of Boone and Crockett proportions. Fred said he got his best look at the right beam and he thought there were six long tines on it. The bowhunters didn't know how high the antlers would score, but, "It was kinda funny because we talked about getting the state record," Hofmann said.

At the time, they were dreaming out loud. They were joking about the possibility of one of them getting that buck, hoping it would happen, but not really expecting it to. They had no idea what hunting season would bring. The comments they made then have new meaning now.

By being persistent, by passing up smaller bucks and being able to take advantage of the opportunity when it arrived, Fred Hofmann did eventually bag that buck with bow and arrow. It is a new state record among typical bow kills. What's so amazing is that at the time Hofmann arrowed the buck, he didn't think it was the one he and Burkhart had seen months earlier. The buck had more points than he thought, with 7 on the right instead of 6 and 10 on the left. The rack's final official score was 186 5/8. The gross score was an amazing 201 4/8.

The previous state record typical in the archery category was a 12-pointer that Phil Hovde of River Falls arrowed in St. Croix County during 1990. Those antlers scored 177 1/8.

Although the record buck is Hofmann's best, by far, that he's taken with bow and arrow, it's certainly not the only decent whitetail he has downed with an arrow. At 29 years of age, Fred said he's been bowhunting for 13 years. His interest in archery was sparked at the age of 15 when he was given a Browning recurve bow by his former brother-in-law Jerry Hoerman. He hunted with that bow for a couple of years before getting a new one.

Fred collected a trio of bucks previously that were a few inches shy of the Pope and Young minimum of 125. He tagged an 11-pointer during the late 1980s, a nice 8-point with an 18 1/2-inch inside spread during late December of 1991 and a 10-pointer on November 7, 1992. He's taken a total of about a dozen whitetails with archery equipment.

Fred Hofmann of Antigo, Wisconsin, with the new state record typical bow kill. The 17-pointer had a final official score of 186 5/8. The buck was 4 1/2-years-old and had a dressed weight of 222 pounds. (Photo by Fred Hofmann)

He said he likes bowhunting for deer much better than hunting them with firearms and also takes it more seriously.

"Bowhunting is more relaxing," Hofmann said. "It's fun to sit out there and watch deer and not see other hunters. There's more of an opportunity to figure deer out. It's also more challenging.

"I normally hunt three to five days a week during bow season. I don't hunt weekends because there's a lot of disturbance from other hunters. The rut is my favorite time to hunt. I always take a week off work to hunt during the rut."

Fred said he spends a lot of time shooting his bow, too. He hunts with a 75 pound pull Darton Excel bow now. He usually participates in 3-D shoots all summer. Although he didn't take part in 3-D shoots as much as normal last year, he did a lot of practice at home.

As hunting season approaches, he does as much scouting as possible to locate bucks and find out what they are doing. Shining is part of his scouting, but he admits that he does it as much because he likes to see deer as anything else. He doesn't hunt some of the areas where he spotlights. Only occasionally is he lucky enough to spot a big buck in an area he hunts, as he was last summer.

Hofmann said he saw a total of six bucks last summer while shining that had racks large enough to qualify for Pope and Young records (at least 125), but they were spread out over a large area. A big 8-pointer with a rack that Fred figured would score close to 140 was one of the P&Y contenders he saw while shining. He saw it again while hunting during mid-October. He said he would have taken that whitetail, if it had given him a good shot, but the buck was too far away on the only occasion their paths crossed.

Fred was sitting on the ground that evening. He was primarily scouting, but he took his bow and arrows with him. It was in a different location than where he ended up claiming the state record deer. He was scouting the location because while shining he had seen other bucks besides the 8-pointer and the sign indicated a much bigger buck lived there.

"There were a lot of nice rubs in the area," he said. "Standing in one spot, I could see 50 rubs. I set up downwind from them in a brushpile. When the 8-pointer came through, he was 50 yards away."

Hofmann said the maximum distance he will take shots at deer while bowhunting is 35 yards. He has one sight pin on his bow that is dead-on from 15 to 25 yards. His 27-inch, 2117 Easton aluminum arrows have a flat trajectory due to the heavy draw weight he shoots. Although his bow is not an overdraw model, Fred said his arrow rest sits back a little bit further than normal. His broadheads of choice are Thunderhead 125s.

The state record holder said he spent a lot of time hunting the area where he saw the big 8-point early in the season. He had another tree stand already positioned along the edge of a field about a half mile from where he saw that buck. Hofmann sat in that stand the first evening he bowhunted during 1994, which was during September, and he had a bachelor group of five bucks walk out in front of him.

The biggest of the five was a 9-pointer that he guessed would score about 110. It and a 7-pointer were sparring 15 yards from his stand that evening. He enjoyed watching them, but had no interest in ending his hunt so early in the season by shooting one of them.

Although Fred saw rubs and tracks that were made by a monster buck in that area and other people reported seeing a bruiser there, Hofmann himself never saw the deer. He didn't do any hunting early in the season where he and his partner had seen the booner during August because he couldn't find any sign confirming the deer was still in the vicinity. Big deer leave big tracks and eventually big rubs. It's not unusual for a mature buck to change habits and habitat after they shed their velvet. Fred figured that's what happened with the unforgettable whitetail he had seen in the spotlight.

But he didn't give up on the location. He checked it periodically, hoping to find some indication the booner was still there or had returned. In late October he finally found what he was looking for near a stand he had hunted from the year before. The trophy buck had recently left sign of his presence in the area.

"There was a line of eight scrapes and a huge rub by the eighth scrape," Hofmann said. "The rub was on a tree that was about as big around as a coffee can. It had to be an eight inch tree. The rub was at chest height and some of the tines had hit the tree as high as my chin. I saw his tracks in there several times. It was obvious the deer that made them was big!"

Seeing that sign got Hofmann fired up. He then knew he still had a chance of seeing the big buck again. The time was approaching when big bucks are most active. That's why he enjoys bowhunting so much during that period.

Fred said he had eight stands up to give him a number of options about where to hunt based on wind direction and deer activity. He also doesn't like to hunt a stand more than once a week. Hofmann was using corn as bait near three of his stands to help keep does nearby. The does, in turn, would attract bucks. He said he doesn't put out bait until at least October 15 to avoid attracting bears.

The property he was hunting is owned by a lumber company and is open to public hunting. He had been hunting that parcel for about five years. That's where he arrowed the 10-pointer scoring about 120 on November 7, 1992. That buck exhibited excellent antler growth for its age (2 1/2 years old) and weighed 155 pounds.

By November 7 of 1994 Hofmann still hadn't seen the buck he wanted, but he wasn't worried. He could concentrate on hunting during the last week of the season since he didn't have to work. He said he likes morning hunting the best during that week.

"If a hot doe goes through, you can watch one buck after another follow her scent all day long," Fred said. And he knew a doe in heat could be the ticket to seeing the special buck that roamed those woods. On the morning of November 10 it finally happened.

He had been in his tree stand about an hour when he heard a grunt. The sound tipped him off that a buck was courting a doe nearby. The doe came in first. He got his first glimpse of the buck in a clearing about 50 yards away. He got a good enough look at the deer's antlers at that point that he decided to take him, if he could.

It was immediately obvious that the rack was a good one, but he did not recognize those antlers as the ones he had seen covered in velvet 2 1/2 months earlier. Part of the reason may be that the buck had his head down trailing the doe most of the time. The elevated position Fred was in also gave him a different perspective. Once Fred made up

When Hofmann saw the big racked buck on November 10, 1994, he didn't think it was the same one he saw in the spotlight months earlier. However, he immediately knew it was a whitetail he wanted. (Photo by Fred Hofmann)

his mind the buck was a shooter, he didn't spend much time looking at the antlers. He concentrated on making a killing shot.

As the buck approached, Hofmann gripped his bow, waiting for the right moment to come to full draw. He made his move when the white-tail's head went behind a six inch maple tree. He was pleased that he got the arrow back without being detected. By then the doe had moved off behind him. He knew if the buck followed, he wouldn't be able to shoot because there were no openings in that direction. So Fred decided to take his shot as the buck approached.

When the deer was 15 yards away, Hofmann released, with his sight pin on the left side of its chest as it quartered toward him. There was a loud crack when the arrow connected.

The trophy buck had a body to match its antlers. The carcass had a dressed weight of 222 pounds. (Photo by Fred Hofmann)

"It looked like there was a lot of arrow sticking out when he ran off," Fred said. "I got concerned about how much penetration there was. I thought there was about 10 inches. I heard him going full blast, then nothing. I didn't know if he simply went out of hearing, stopped, slowed to a walk or went down."

It was 6:50 a.m. when Hofmann arrowed the buck. He decided to get help before trailing it. He had a telephone in his van and he called friend Bill (Willy) Bostwick at 7:30.

The first thing Willy asked when Fred picked him up was, "Is it the big one?"

"I don't think so," was Hofmann's response.

When they returned to the hunting area, it didn't take the pair long to find the buck. It had died on its feet after running 100 yards, bowling over a balsam tree when it fell. The broadhead had gone through the left shoulder and imbedded in the heart.

Once they reached the fallen deer, it soon became obvious the whitetail was the big one after all. That's when Fred really got excited. As he and Bill Burkhart realized when they first saw the buck, he knew the antlers were of Boone and Crockett proportions. He was in for even more excitement when it sunk in that the rack was a new state record by a wide margin.

Bill Burkhart was working on construction the day Fred scored. Hofmann and Bostwick loaded the buck in the back of Bostwick's pickup truck to show Burkhart the trophy. Burkhart's first thought when he saw the buck was that Bostwick had hit it with his truck. He had killed a big 10-pointer scoring 159 that way the year before.

Burkhart was obviously pleased that his partner had gotten the monster buck they both first glimpsed in the beam of a spotlight. Although work prohibited Bill from hunting as much as he would like in the fall, he had taken a bragging size buck with bow and arrow himself four years earlier. The 10-point scored 161.

Hofmann's buck proved to be 4 1/2 years old and had a dressed weight of 222 pounds. It's not likely that Hofmann and Burkhart will see another buck like it in their spotlight during the near future. However, I'm willing to bet they will be out there trying anyway. They like to see deer even if they aren't of state record proportions.

Chapter 20

The Importance of Antlerless Harvest

It's obvious there are too many deer in an area when desirable trees can no longer grow. Under most circumstances, it would be impossible to determine whether whitetails are having such a dramatic impact on their habitat, but it's obvious where deer exclosures have been erected. Exclosures are nothing more than small patches of ground that are fenced to keep deer out.

Vegetation protected from whitetails inside exclosures grows normally, while trees and plants growing outside the exclosure continue

Michigan Department of Natural Resources Forester Mike Zuidema standing next to an exclosure (a fenced area where whitetails have been prevented from feeding). Healthy saplings have grown inside the exclosure where they have been protected from deer.

to be influenced by the animals. After a period of years, it's possible to see how much impact whitetails have on the plant community by comparing what's growing inside exclosures with what's outside. Man, is there a difference in locations where whitetails are overabundant.

Several deer exclosures I saw recently in southern counties of Michigan's Upper Peninsula are prime examples. Michigan Department of Natural Resources Forester Mike Zuidema took me on a tour to show them to me. I was amazed at what a dramatic difference there was.

Zuidema has his hands behind a pair of puny saplings outside the exclosure, which are sure to be eaten by deer when they get bigger.

The first stop was at an exclosure erected in 1986 under a canopy of mature hemlock and white pine trees. Over the nine years the fencing had been in place, thick growth of young hemlock and white pine trees had established themselves inside. Some of them were two to three feet high. Outside the exclosure the ground looked bare, with the exception of a carpet of pine needles. However, if you looked closely, you could see tiny hemlock sprouts. The chances of survival for those tiny trees was not good. Deer are sure to eat them when they get big enough to be noticed.

The story was the same at the next exclosure, which was in a small opening where the sun shines periodically. Mike said there was a carpet of birch and hemlock saplings in that opening when he put the exclosure up. When I was there, the ground outside the fencing appeared barren. Inside the fence, there was thick growth of pin cherry, birch and hemlock. The young deciduous trees were at least 10 feet tall.

The third stop was at an exclosure erected in an opening during 1991 after a stand of maple and white birch trees had been cut. You guessed it. There was excellent growth of saplings inside the exclosure

The failure of hunters to remove enough antlerless deer from many herds results in an unhealthy situation for the habitat, the animals and hunters.

and hard-to-see, stunted sprouts outside. With full sunlight, plenty of grass had been able to grow at that site, but not much else.

When deer numbers get too high, as they obviously are in those areas, they not only prevent regrowth of forests, they prevent development of a future food supply and cover for themselves. Such a situation is not good for either deer or deer hunters. Poorly nourished whitetails are small in size and have lousy antler development. In extreme cases, the habitat deteriorates enough to cause a major die-off, resulting in the presence of few deer.

In most cases, failure to remove enough antlerless deer from the population on an annual basis is responsible for such a sad situation. The only way to control whitetails is to harvest a portion of the does in the herd each year. If that isn't done, the animals' reproductive potential is so high that they invariably eat themselves out of house and home. The more hunters who understand that and do their part to take does when they can, the better. The key is to control the population in the first place so negative impacts on the habitat don't develop. The whitetails that remain will be healthier, and the quality of hunting will be better, too.

The first deer I shot with both gun and bow many years ago were does. I was proud of taking them because connecting on any whitetail was a challenge then. After I went through a couple of years without filling tags, those antlerless animals broke the ice for me. I've taken my share of bucks since then, but I still shoot antlerless deer (does and fawns) today on a regular basis. I am proud of it, although for different reasons.

The bucks still manage to elude me now and then like they used to, so taking any deer is sometimes as challenging as it once was. More importantly though, I now understand the value of harvesting antlerless deer in the proper management of whitetails. I'm proud that my decision to shoot does and fawns during recent years is motivated by my

Every hunter is also a manager. The whitetails he or she chooses to shoot will have a bearing on the future health of the herd.

From a management perspective, the removal of does and fawns by hunters is more important than the harvest of bucks, despite the fact most hunters put more emphasis on shooting bucks.

interest in exercising my role as a deer manager as well as a hunter, even though the kill may not be challenging.

During a recent autumn in my home state of Michigan, for example, the only deer I shot was antlerless. Toward the end of gun season I collected a button buck under a bonus permit. I was trying for a doe and thought the whitetail was a yearling doe when I shot it. Nonetheless, from a management perspective taking that deer was better than taking either of the two antlered bucks I could have shot.

I passed up a spikehorn and forkhorn, both of which were probably 1 1/2 years old. The bucks that I let go will be more valuable to me and any other hunter who might see them as 2 1/2-year-olds because they will have full-fledged racks. As older bucks, they will probably play a more important role in breeding, too.

The young buck I did shoot was more expendable because there was a chance he might not have survived his first winter in the north country. Fawns, and especially buck fawns, are often the first to die dur-

The best way to insure the presence of trophy bucks like this one in a population of whitetails is to make sure enough antlerless deer are harvested annually.

ing a rough winter. In fact, winter fawn loss can be a significant problem in northern Michigan some years. More on that later.

State and provincial wildlife biologists who set deer hunting seasons and regulations are often viewed as the primary deer managers. They certainly play a very important part in managing deer herds. But each and every hunter is potentially a manager, too. As a whole, they play just as important a role, if not more so, than the biologists. In order for deer herds to be properly managed, harvest quotas set by biologists must be met by hunters. Both types of managers must work together to achieve objectives.

Despite the emphasis placed on the harvesting of bucks among hunters, removal of does from deer populations is actually more important. The willingness of hunters to shoot does and fawns may ultimately decide the fate of hunting for deer in some areas. Besides providing valuable recreation, hunting for deer can be justified as a tool for managing deer herds. Hunters who only kill antlered bucks are not participating in deer management. The removal of antlered bucks plays a small part in determining future population levels of deer.

Not only is the harvest of antlerless deer good whitetail management, it is the best way to produce quality bucks with the biggest racks, too. One of the primary goals of deer management is to keep population levels low enough so there is enough natural food to go around during critical times of the year, such as winter. This increases the potential for healthy herds with little or no stress or starvation losses. Healthy herds consistently produce bucks with the biggest antlers.

There are other benefits of keeping a deer population below the carrying capacity of the habitat. Car deer collisions and crop damage are minimized. Healthy does also produce more fawns that survive than does that are stressed due to overcrowding and malnutrition. High reproductive rates mean that hunters can take more animals without having a negative impact on the herd.

The value of harvesting does to produce quality bucks was demonstrated by Dr. Harry Jacobson, a professor at Mississippi State University's Department of Wildlife and Fisheries, on 18,000 acre Davis Island. Up until the time Jacobson became involved in managing deer on the island, there had been no harvest of antlerless whitetails and intensive harvest of antlered bucks. The resulting population was heavily lopsided in favor of does. Bucks were young with small racks.

Does that sound familiar?

There were also too many whitetails present. Jacobson's goal was to manage for a deer population that was one half of what the habitat could support. He said an ideal sex ratio that would maximize fawn production would be three does per buck.

The harvest of antlerless deer increased steadily each of the first four years of the management program. There was a dip in the number of does taken during the fifth and sixth years because hunters became concerned about removing too many deer. By the end of the program's sixth year, however, hunters saw the management strategy was working and there was renewed support for healthy antlerless harvests.

Even though more deer were being shot by hunters, the remaining does were more productive than they had been before antlerless harvests started. Increased productivity helped offset some of the kill, insuring a good crop of healthy whitetails for the future. At the beginning of the program, for example, the does on Davis Island were carrying an

The presence of spike bucks most often reflects poor nutrition or an unbalanced sex ratio and overpopulation resulting in fawns that were born late—rather than poor genetics.

average of one fawn apiece, with few, if any, doe fawns breeding. Five years later, there was an average of 2.2 fawns per doe, with up to 30 percent of doe fawns producing offspring.

A better balance in the herd's sex ratio had a positive influence on peak breeding, too, moving it up by about a month. When the herd was out of balance, peak breeding occurred between January 14 and 22. After 10 years of antlerless harvests, breeding took place between December 9 and January 13, with the peak during December 22. The earlier does are bred, the earlier fawns are born, resulting in a good crop of healthy youngsters. The bucks among them are also more likely to have branched antlers as yearlings.

Jacobson's research has shown that the presence of a high percentage of spike bucks in a deer population is more often either a reflection of poor nutrition brought about by overcrowding or bucks that are born late in the year, rather than poor genetics. Lopsided sex ratios favoring does often produce a higher percentage of late born fawns because there aren't enough bucks to breed does during their first estrus cycle. When too many deer are present, bucks don't often get enough protein in their spring and summer diets (13-18 percent) for optimum antler development.

Jacobson cited an example to illustrate what impact a reduction in protein levels in the diet of a buck can have on antler growth. As a yearling eating natural forage this particular buck grew 4-point antlers. The deer was put in captivity the following year and fed a diet containing 10 percent protein. As a 2 1/2-year-old, that buck grew spikes. When returned to a 16 percent protein diet the following year, the buck grew a 12-point rack.

Average weights of yearling bucks on Davis Island increased as a result of antlerless harvests. Before the program started, yearling bucks averaged 95 pounds. After five years, they averaged 135 pounds. There was a corresponding improvement in antlers, too. Average beam lengths of yearling bucks went from four to seven inches. Beam lengths among 2 1/2-year-olds averaged 16 inches after 10 years compared to 11 1/2 inches earlier.

By the sixth year of the program the buck harvest was voluntarily restricted to animals with beam lengths of 13 inches and/or a 13-inch spread between antler beams. After three years, 80 percent of the bucks taken by hunters were 2 1/2 years old or older. Prior to the antler size limit, 80 percent of the buck harvest was made up of yearlings.

Some quality (trophy) bucks were taken on Davis Island after 10 years of antlerless harvests. Jacobson said about 40 bucks that weighed 200 pounds or better and had beam lengths of at least 20 inches had been recorded. He added that the highest scoring rack had measurements totaling 156. And that's in spite of the fact that most of the island's bucks were still represented by young age classes, with a small percentage reaching 3 1/2 and 4 1/2 years of age.

There's some valuable lessons to be learned by deer hunters everywhere from this example. At the top of the list: the way to balance a deer herd and produce quality bucks at the same time is to harvest at least as many does as bucks. In some cases, it may help to remove more does than bucks annually, as was practiced on Davis Island. The

Hunters can increase their time afield and hunting opportunities by participating in special hunts on which the harvest of antlerless deer is emphasized to reduce crop damage or control deer populations such as those on hard-to-reach islands.

average annual deer harvest on the island for a seven-year period was 452, according to Jacobson, 235 of which were does and 217 bucks. Intensive harvests of does and fawns permit the taking of more deer, resulting in higher hunter success. At the same time, overall quality of the herd is improved or maintained.

On the Palmyra Hunt Club, for example, which is one of the hunting clubs on Davis Island, the average annual deer kill on their 5,000 acres was 43 whitetails before the management program started. During the 10 years that antlerless deer were actively taken, the average annual kill more than tripled to 155. The harvest during those years included 84 does and 71 bucks.

It's important to note that although the antlerless harvest went up dramatically, there was also a 60 percent increase in the number of bucks bagged during those years than before. And despite the in-

234   THE IMPORTANCE OF ANTLERLESS HARVEST

creased buck harvest, the future availability of bucks to hunters continued to improve. The bottom line, according to Jacobson, is that the removal of excess does makes room for more bucks. This also proves that shooting does is necessary to produce the best buck hunting.

There are instances where hunters can increase their time afield and get access to locations they might not otherwise be able to hunt by participating in deer management through the harvest of antlerless deer. Farmers who are suffering crop damage from deer, for instance, are more willing to grant permission to hunt to those who will shoot does than those who are only interested in bucks. In areas where multiple tags are available, hunters may be able to take one to several antlerless animals as a management measure, then try for a buck. On Lake Michigan's South Fox and North Manitou Islands, for example, hunters have been permitted to shoot as many as three deer at various times, only one of which could be an antlered buck.

The block permit program was initiated in Michigan a number of years ago as a means of getting hunters to help farmers control whitetails that are raiding their crops. Block permits are only valid for antlerless animals during state hunting seasons. The permits are purchased from the DNR by farmers with problems. The farmers then can issue the tags to hunters. Deer shot under block permits don't count as part of the annual bag limit.

A total of 12,770 antlerless deer were reported taken under block permits in Michigan by the third year of the program, according to DNR Big Game Specialist Ed Langenau. He said 1,806 of those does and fawns were taken by bowhunters, 9,735 were collected during gun season and 1,229 were bagged during the black powder season. The year before, 14,274 antlerless deer were tagged with block permits; 2,060 during bow seasons, 10,818 in gun season and 1,396 on the muzzleloader hunt.

Hunters who fill block permits can keep the meat themselves, give it to farmers or donate it to a program to help feed needy families.

One point that I want to emphasize about the value of shooting antlerless deer is that there is absolutely nothing wrong with shooting fawns or young-of-the-year. In fact, shooting fawns may be more desirable than tagging adult does, at least in northern states and Canada, because four- to six-month old deer are the most expendable segment of the population. In areas where long, cold winters are common, fawns are the most susceptible to malnutrition and starvation losses. It is far better that the animals be removed by hunters before critical periods than to lose them to starvation.

Food that fawns eat is wasted, in a sense, if they end up dying. That browse better benefits the resource if it is consumed by an adult that survives. It's up to hunters as deer managers to help make that happen.

Harvesting young deer is an important part of deer management in northern states and Canada. There's nothing wrong with shooting "fawns."

The managers for state and provincial agencies could also help by offering incentives to hunters who choose to harvest fawns.

The value of harvesting fawns was tested and proven at Michigan's Cusino Wildlife Research Station, which is operated by the DNR. A herd of whitetails in a square mile enclosure was manipulated to simulate intensive cropping of young animals by removing them from the enclosure on an annual basis. The most productive, prime-age deer were retained.

Under that type of management, the herd nearly doubled annually, according to DNR Wildlife Research Biologist John Ozoga, which represents a 30 to 40 percent greater rate of production than normal. John said a spring herd of 40 whitetails regularly increased to 75 or 80 by fall every year.

"Needless to say," John wrote in a report on the project, "selective cropping of fawns would make particularly good sense on northern range, where limited food and/or cover resources necessitates carrying smaller overwinter deer herds. Since many young deer do not survive their first year in any case, their harvest has minimal effect on the population as a whole."

Part of understanding the importance of antlerless harvests is grasping the folly of bucks-only hunting. The reproductive potential of healthy whitetail does, for example, is so high that if none are harvested the pop-

Bucks-only hunting is poor management.

ulation soon reaches a point where there are too many for the available food supply. When there's no longer enough food to go around, malnutrition and starvation losses occur. The reproductive rate also declines in an effort to compensate for overcrowded conditions.

Since bucks, and especially buck fawns, have higher nutritional needs than does, due to their larger size, they are hardest hit when competition is severe for food. As a result, a higher proportion of bucks are lost to starvation than does. Due to bucks only hunting, there's already more does than bucks in the population. Starvation losses further offset the sex ratio.

Surviving bucks have too many does to breed, adding to their stress. Antler development and body weights are often poor for bucks in overpopulated situations. Late breeding and late born fawns are other symptoms. None of these symptoms are desirable.

For a specific example of how bucks-only hunting works, let's start with a healthy herd of 150 adult whitetails, consisting of 100 does and 50 bucks. Let's assume the does produce an average of 1.5 fawns apiece the first year and 1.25 every year thereafter, considering the presence of non-breeding doe fawns. For convenience sake, let's assume an equal number of bucks and does are born and hunters remove 75 percent of the available bucks each year. The accompanying chart shows what could happen over a span of 10 years. By spring of the eleventh year, our paper herd would include 9,445 whitetails—many more than we started with.

Amazingly, the buck-to-doe ratio has varied little over that 10-year period, even though three-fourths of the bucks were removed every year, with the ratio remaining close to a pair of does for every buck. The number of bucks in the population continues to increase. So does the number shot by hunters annually. One of the problems with this scenario is the majority of bucks are young animals, too young to have antlers. Before hunting season opened on the tenth year, only 593 out of 3,855 bucks (15 percent) would have antlers.

In reality, the percentage of antlered deer in the population would have been even lower. On paper, the majority of bucks were removed from the herd every year, most of which would have been button bucks. A true-to-life bucks-only hunting situation would have only removed 75 percent of the antlered bucks each year. This promotes a high harvest of bucks as soon as they grow their first set of antlers, which is exactly what happens in many areas.

Hunters see a high proportion of antlerless deer and few bucks with antlers. Many hunters assume most of the baldies are does, but a respectable number of those antlerless deer are actually button bucks that won't be legal targets until the following year. What the table shows, and what most hunters don't realize, is that a significant number of button bucks can be harvested every year under antlerless permits, still leaving plenty of bucks for future years. In fact, if more button bucks (antlerless deer) are taken in the place of antlered bucks (yearlings) there will be an increase in mature bucks for the future.

Something else many hunters fail to realize about the bucks-only scenario is that the population starts trying to compensate for too many animals long before the herd size of about 10,000 is reached in 10 years. The herd will increase and reproduction will remain healthy as long as there's enough food for all of the deer. After the carrying capacity of the habitat is exceeded, things start falling apart. Assuming the habitat our paper herd is living on has a carrying capacity of 1,000 deer, the table with this chapter would lose its validity after the fifth year.

Many antlerless deer that hunters see are button bucks like this one. Button bucks can be included as part of the antlerless harvest without having a major impact on the number of antlered bucks available the following year.

After the habitat can no longer sustain the number of deer present, average weights of deer declines, starvation occurs, fawn production and survival nose-dives. Does will continue having fawns, but if does are malnourished, fawns won't be as well developed as they otherwise would be. Many of them will die soon after birth because they are too small and weak to stand or nurse. As mentioned earlier, when food supplies are reduced, buck fawns are more susceptible to starvation than young does. When that starts happening, it's possible to lose a high percentage of bucks before they get old enough to develop antlers, whether or not any are taken by hunters. Under those circumstances, annual recruitment of yearling bucks may be low and the bulk of the population may consist of does.

By keeping deer numbers below the habitat's carrying capacity, those problems can be avoided. As already mentioned, the only way to do that is to shoot antlerless deer. A certain number of does are born every year. A population will continue to increase if fewer does are removed than the number born. Harvest of does has to equal production to keep a herd stable.

The removal of equal numbers of bucks and does from a population is an ideal way to manage a herd. If you want to manage for a high proportion of mature bucks, more does than bucks should be shot annually. The examples from Dr. Harry Jacobson's management in Mississippi that were mentioned earlier clearly illustrate how that works.

Projected Deer Population Under Bucks Only Hunting With 1.25 Fawns Per Doe, 50/50 Sex Ratio of Fawns and Harvest of 75 Percent of Bucks

Year	Does	Bucks	Fawns	Buck Harvest	Buck/Does
1	100	50	37	37	1/2
2	175	88	150	66	1/1.99
3	284	132	219	99	1/2.1
4	461	211	355	158	1/2.2
5	749	341	576	256	1/2.2
6	1,217	553	936	415	1/2.2
7	1,977	898	1,521	673	1/2.2
8	3,212	1,460	2,471	1,095	1/2.2
9	5,219	2,372	4,015	1,779	1/2.2
10	8,481	3,855	6,524	2,891	1/2.2
11	SPRING POPULATION: 9,445				

Chapter 21

Celebrity Deer Hunt

New York Yankees third baseman Wade Boggs set the tone for his December deer hunt in Michigan before it even started. We were on the way to the Wildlife Place rifle range to test-fire his 200th Anniversary Commemorative Remington .30-06 when he told me, "You're looking at the luckiest man on the planet. When it comes to deer hunting, I'm one of the luckiest men alive."

I was going to be his guide and I told him we could use all of the luck he was able to muster. I knew there were some tremendous whitetail bucks on the property we would be hunting because the Wildlife Place manages all of its holdings specifically for the production of trophy bucks. I had seen some of the big antlered bucks on previous hunts, and so had other guides.

However, this was the last buck hunt of the season and there weren't as many mature bucks on the 900 acres as there had been earlier in the season. Those that were left were super shy, and they would be tough to see. It didn't take long to find out my concern was unnecessary, however.

Boggs brought enough luck with him for the other two celebrities on the hunt as well as himself. The other hunt-ers were Yankees teammate and pitcher Jimmy Key and Virginia Commander, a

New York Yankees third baseman Wade Boggs displays his good luck hunting charm. He claims he's the luckiest man on the planet when it comes to whitetail hunting. His success shows he could be right.

New York publisher. All three members of the party scored on trophy bucks during the hunt. Boggs got the one with the highest scoring rack, but not by much.

After the scope sights on all three rifles were squared away, we took advantage of some of the best hunting time of the day by going to blinds overlooking feeding areas. Most hunting at the Wildlife Place is done from blinds because it's much easier to judge the antlers of a feeding whitetail with binoculars from a secure position that offers a good view of the surroundings. Emphasis is put on passing up young bucks and taking mature animals, so it's important that hunters and guides know what's going to be shot before the trigger is touched.

Aggressive antlerless harvests are an important part of deer management at the Wildlife Place in an effort to control population size and growth as well as the ratio of bucks to does. A sex ratio of 1 to 1 is the goal, but it may vary from one year to the next. At any rate, close to 50 percent of the whitetail population on Wildlife Place's three properties totaling close to 3,000 acres are bucks. Hunters there normally get to look at a lot of antlers, even though many of them may not be what the hunters are looking for.

That basically describes Wade's first evening of hunting, with one exception. We did see a lot of bucks and they weren't what we were looking for, but there was this unique 10-pointer that Boggs really did want to shoot. However, I discouraged him because the rack wasn't of the caliber he wanted. When we started hunting, he told me he was looking for a buck that would score in the 160s.

I estimated that the 10-point he was interested in would only score in the 130s. What set that whitetail's rack apart from the others we saw that evening was the shape of the second tine (G2s) on both beams. They were each long and curved backward like the beam tips of elk antlers. Neither of us had seen a whitetail rack like it. There's no question that buck would have made a nice mount, but I knew we could do much better.

Wade looked longingly at that buck through his rifle's scope several times during the 30 minutes he was in front of us, admiring his headgear. To his credit, he didn't consider pulling the trigger. There aren't many places in the United States that hunters or guides would consider passing up a buck like that.

We saw at least 15 bucks during the evening, three of which had 10 points, including the one with the curved G2s, and a wide-antlered 9-point. One of the 10s had heavy antlers and was close to what Wade was looking for, but it had a broken brow tine, which eliminated him from serious consideration. I was surprised to learn that Jimmy, Virginia and their guides didn't see as many deer as we did when we compared notes back at the guest house, but I shouldn't have been. Wade was obviously right about his deer hunting luck and it had kicked in.

A gold-plated buck that Wade wears on a chain around his neck is one of the important good luck charms he relies on for deer hunting. He got it as a gift from former Boston Red Sox player Eric Hetzel from Louisiana five years earlier, and he's worn it ever since when hunting. The good luck charm paid off in a big way the following morning.

We went back to the same blind we had been in the evening before, which is on the edge of a steep oak ridge. We saw the same wide 9-point-

Wade Boggs approaches the trophy 10-point he shot while stand hunting with the author as his guide at the Wildlife Place.

er that paid us a visit the previous evening, another nice 9-point and a mature buck with only one antler. Then about 9:00 a.m., a beautiful 10-pointer emerged from a clump of thick saplings about 60 yards in front of us and started to feed. After looking the rack over through my Nikon binoculars, I was convinced this was the buck Wade wanted.

The beams were long and wide. Two tines on each side were also long. I estimated the rack would score in the 160s, and I gave Wade the go-ahead to shoot. I figured he would be anxious to take such a fine buck, but he wasn't sure the deer was as good as I thought. Fortunately, the buck was content feeding where he was for a while as I tried to convince Wade to shoot the whitetail.

All I recall saying every time he asked me a question about the buck's rack is, "Shoot him!"

By the time I talked Boggs into taking the deer, a tree was covering its chest cavity. All it had to do for its vitals to clear the tree was move

Wade Boggs with his 10-point buck. The antlers had a gross score of 168.

Guide Dan Soldan points out a buck to New York Yankees pitcher Jimmy Key while hunting from a blind.

ahead about a foot. We waited anxiously for a long time for that to happen, but it never did. When the buck moved, he turned around and went back the way he had come, re-entering the thick saplings. I thought that was the last we were going to see of that buck. If I were hunting with anyone else it probably would have been, but Wade's exceptional luck kicked in again.

Seconds after entering the saplings, the buck came back out and walked along the edge from left to right. More tense moments elapsed, during which Wade had to move to another window in the blind, before the buck finally stopped in a position where a clear shot was possible. Boggs is obviously good under pressure because he made his shot count. Once he made up his mind to shoot, he didn't want that buck to get away. Fortunately, it didn't.

The rack was as good as I thought it was. The gross score, which is how deer at the Wildlife Place are field judged, was 168. Both beams were 25 inches long, the inside spread was 20 2/8 inches, and four tines were close to 10 inches or more in length. The carcass weighed 195 pounds in the round. The whitetail was 4 1/2 or 5 1/2 years old.

Jimmy and guide Dan Soldan saw what they thought was a high-tined 8-pointer that morning, along with some smaller bucks. Dan gave Jimmy an okay to shoot the biggest buck, but the pitcher decided to wait on the chance he might see something better during the rest of the hunt. He did see a heavy-beamed buck during a drive that afternoon, but he was unable to get a shot at it before it was gone. Drives are sometimes used to fill the time between morning and evening stints in blinds at the Wildlife Place, especially late in the season. This tactic often gives hunters a look at bucks that are seldom seen from blinds, but it's not always possible to get a shot at them on drives either, as Jimmy's experience proved.

Wade and I saw some respectable bucks during the drives, but nothing better than the one he already had. We did see one that was at least as good. However, if he took a second buck, he wanted it to be in the 170s. I knew whitetails of that caliber were on the property, but it was impossible to know if we would see one.

On the second evening it was Virginia's turn to score from a blind. A shot came from the blind she and guide Dan Vander sys occupied at 4:10 p.m. After dark we all admired the results—a massive antlered 10-pointer. Jimmy felt confident that buck was the one he almost got a shot at during one of the drives. The antlers scored 166, only 1 3/8-of-an-inch less than Wade's, and the deer weighed 218 pounds.

The circumferences on the beams from Virginia's deer were impressive. Most of the measurements were over five inches. The greatest circumference was 6 5/8 inches. Tine and beam lengths were also good and the inside spread was 18 inches.

Virginia made an 80 yard shot on the trophy buck with her 7 mm magnum, tipping the big buck right over as it was standing broadside in a field. Her guide said they had seen some smaller bucks and a group of does before the big buck arrived.

That evening Jimmy and his guide also saw some good bucks, including a good 10-pointer that the guide guessed would score about 145. Soldan videotaped that deer as well as some others. All of us got a chance to view the video after dinner. There was no question that whitetail was a good one, but Key was still holding out for something better.

Wade and I spent the evening in the blind Jimmy and his guide had been hunting, which is where Key passed up the exceptional 8-pointer. We happened to see that same buck, and we were both impressed with the antlers. In addition to the 8 main tines, we noticed a sticker point coming off of the G2 on the left side. I figured the rack would measure in the 150s.

That was the best buck we saw for the evening, but we also got a look at a nice 9-point and a serious fight between two smaller whitetails. The turf was really flying as the pair dug their hooves in for traction to push each other around. The smallest deer, both in body and antler size, was the most aggressive. He appeared to win the contest. The bigger buck eventually broke away from the fight and took off running.

Virginia Commander with her trophy whitetail. The heavy antlers of the buck had a gross score of 166 and the deer weighed 218 pounds.

The following morning, Jimmy and his guide returned to the blind where he passed up the big 8 with the sticker point. We were all hoping Key would kill that buck, if he saw it again. Wade and I were a couple of hundred yards away in the blind where he had shot his 10-pointer. As it got light, another 10-pointer appeared. The rack was smaller than on the one Wade shot, but it was still decent.

That buck wasn't in front of us for long before it wandered off toward where Jimmy was posted. Minutes later, we heard Jimmy shoot. We thought he might have taken the buck we saw go his way, but realized he could have shot at any number of other bucks, including the

Jimmy Key with the 10-pointer he eventually shot after passing it up on his second day of hunting. The whitetail's rack had a gross score of 152 and the carcass weighed 199 pounds.

one he had passed up previously. When we met up with them later, we found out he nailed the one he let go before.

The antlers proved to have two sticker points instead of one, making it a 10-point. One of the brow tines was forked in addition to the ex-

Wade Boggs, Virginia Commander and Jimmy Key with the trio of terrific bucks they shot late in the season while stand hunting at Michigan's Wildlife Place.

tra tine off the G2. Jimmy wanted a 10-pointer and that's what he got. The rack ended up scoring 152.

The beams were 23 6/8 and 24 6/8 inches long. Inside spread was 19 2/8 inches. The longest tine measured 12 2/8 inches in length and three more points were close to 10 inches long. It was a fine mature buck weighing 199 pounds, to add to the other pair that had been taken.

I later learned from Wade that before the hunt that morning, Jimmy told his teammate that he planned on being back to the guest house eating breakfast by 8:00 a.m. He certainly could have made it. He pulled the trigger at 7:50. Jimmy and his guide told us that the trophy buck he shot was feeding with a group of deer after it got light enough to see. Neither of them saw the buck come in.

There was at least one similarity between Jimmy and Wade's kills. The buck started to walk away before Jimmy made up his mind to shoot, walking into the woods to the left. The buck soon walked back in the open though and Jimmy shot it soon afterward. Dan captured the kill on video. Some interesting conversation between Jimmy and Dan was also captured on the tape.

During the remainder of their hunt, the trio saw some more nice bucks, both from blinds and on drives, but didn't end up shooting anything else. As it turned out, I ended up getting a good look at a 170 class buck Wade would have liked to have shot, but he wasn't with me at the time. We had finished a drive. While Wade joined Virginia Commander and Dan Vander sys to walk out to a nearby road, I backtracked to retrieve my vehicle and drove around to meet them.

I spotted the world class buck from the vehicle while driving. It was with some does that had circled around behind the drivers. The whitetail wore a beautiful 10-point rack similar to the one Wade already had, but it was bigger in a number of ways. The antlers had more mass, longer beams, a wider spread and longer tines. I'm sure they would have measured in the neighborhood of 175.

Nonetheless, the trio of celebrities did extremely well by stand hunting, considering the circumstances. There aren't many places where three hunters could walk away with quality bucks like that on the last hunt of the season. For more information write, call or fax Wildlife Place, Bitely, MI 49309 (616-745-8000) FAX (616-745-9000).

Venison from deer that Boggs, Key and Commander bagged at the Wildlife Place was donated to Sportsmen Against Hunger, a program sponsored in Michigan by Safari Club International, Michigan United Conservation Clubs, Michigan Bow Hunters Association, Ted Nugent World Bowhunters and the United Methodist Men's Club. Under the program, meat from their whitetails was professionally processed and given to needy families.

Index

S

T

V

W